Unread
Pages

Unread Pages
The Silent Struggles Behind Every Success

Marnie Del Beauchamp

Published by Game Changer Publishing

Paperback ISBN: 978-1-961189-97-3
Hardcover ISBN: 978-1-961189-98-0
Digital: ISBN: 978-1-961189-99-7

www.GameChangerPublishing.com

DEDICATION

A legacy to my brave, beautiful daughters, Carla and India, who have always been my WHY. You are my world, and I could not be any prouder of you. Being a mum to you has made the most profound and meaningful impact on my life, more so than I could ever have dreamt of.

To my sweet, precious grandson, Taana, who brightens all our lives. I absolutely adore you. It's so true what they say about being a grandparent and the incredibly special love you share.

And to my parents, now the brightest stars in the sky—you still inspire me each and every day. I love you and miss you with all my heart.

But First

Thank you so much for buying and reading my book. I am so grateful!
To show my appreciation, I'd like to invite you to a welcome
call with me. I'd love your feedback.

Scan the QR Code:

Unread Pages

The Silent Struggles Behind Every Success

Marnie Del Beauchamp

www.GameChangerPublishing.com

Preface

I wrote this book to inspire those brave enough to venture into the unknown—in business and life. To remind you that your past has no significance in your present and that your future has no reflection on your past. The only important moment in your life is now. Now is where the magic happens. Now is when you're truly living. Now is your opportunity to take action.

All it takes to fulfill your dreams is unwavering belief combined with purpose, commitment, and courage to weather the storms you'll encounter along the way. Do not let the fear of failure be your mooring line. Fear and the ensuing self-doubt are what hold 90 percent of people back from living their best life, starting a business, embarking on a new career, or a whole new life journey. It stops them from taking a chance and unleashing their power to achieve whatever it is that they want. But failure is inevitable. We all fail. Life is full of failures if you really think about it. And yet, how often have those failures been permanent? That only happens if you give up.

You can learn a lot from the things that don't work out or go wrong in your life just by reflecting on why and how they happened. Then, use that information to do it better the next time around. Often, that "failure" will be the catalyst for your biggest success.

Excessive fear of failure mostly comes from reliving past experiences and the emotions they elicit. For example, children who grow up in a highly critical environment, with parents or influential adults who have a captious parenting style, will fear failure more acutely. Those who have experienced bullying or a traumatic event and those who have failed at something and wound up feeling humiliated, embarrassed, or upset will also tend to fear failure a lot more. This is because those emotions stay with you beyond the initial incident, and every time you think about doing something new or pushing boundaries outside of your comfort zone, those emotions rise up to remind you how it felt to fail and to stop you from repeating them.

So what you actually fear is the emotion attached to it—the humiliation or shame. Not the failure itself. The past failures become the excuses as to why you aren't working on achieving your goals or making positive changes in your life. By recognising this, you can begin to understand that all you need to do is let go of the past and all events in it. Shift your mindset. Think differently. Because reliving them will not change anything; it will just keep you trapped in past trauma, which is blocking you from reaching your potential.

Just live in the present. Focus on the excitement and anticipation of what you're building. Take baby steps each day, always moving towards your goals, and life will present truly amazing opportunities to you. Be open and ready for them because nothing will stop them but you. You are the only limiting factor in your life. If you don't take the opportunity, it will never become anything, and if you don't believe that you can achieve anything, you won't.

We are never guaranteed a tomorrow; right now is all we can count on. So why aren't you making the most of it? What have you got to lose, really? Explore the possibilities. DWELL in possibility. Life truly is an adventure, and every day is the opportune time to start your new journey. But remember, it's important that you don't expect to stick to what's comfortable and known because you'll be stepping into the uncomfortable and the unknown. This is where you will grow and learn. It's where you're meant to be.

There is no doubt that there will be challenges that will push you, test you, and quite possibly bend you at times. But every time you encounter hardship, it will teach you something new, build resilience, and instil more confidence and trust in yourself.

Always remember:

- The decisions you make are yours alone.
- The words you speak are yours alone.
- The thoughts you have are yours alone.
- The emotions you feel are yours alone.
- The feelings you choose are yours alone.
- The path you take is yours alone.

It's ALL yours. Decide wisely. No matter what happens, you have the ability to control what your next step is. Don't just live in hope, that won't get you anywhere. As Nike says, JUST DO IT!

Take action and do what makes you happy.

This book is my gift to you to prove that there are no boundaries, no excuses. We all f*#k up, and we all fail, but if you want it bad enough… go get it.

Table of Contents

Introduction

Before we begin, let me just explain my waves analogy.

"Life comes in waves." I'm sure you have all heard that saying. Sometimes, the waves are small ripples; other times, they are the magnitude of a tidal wave that will knock you completely off your feet, drag you relentlessly to the bottom, and thrash you around like a tumble dryer. The waves sometimes come at you with unrelenting impact or smash you out of the blue, catching you completely unawares. But no matter how many times you're dumped, thrashed around, and spat out the other side, you must always try to find a way to make it back to shore. Whether you swim against the tide or allow the surge to drag you out, conserve your energy to swim back in when you have the strength. Sometimes, you just need to embrace the ebb and flow, holding your head above water and feeling the pressure of the ups and downs until you have the clarity to find a new direction back to safety.

The energy of the ocean is immense. As is the energy of life.

The ocean can teach us some important life lessons.

1. Freedom. Don't live anchored down in expectation, responsibility, or limitations that don't align with your happiness and purpose.

2. Fearlessness. Don't be afraid to make waves when following opportunities and building your future. Make sure you're seen.

3. Fluidity. Life and business are an ever-changing frequency. It can be tumultuous, but it can also be calm. So be patient with the changes as they come and go.

4. Purpose. Every action creates a reaction—cause and effect. So consider your every action as one of intention and meaning.

5. Peacefulness. While it's inevitable you'll experience storms, they never last forever. So be grateful and know that everything will calm down in time.

6. Vibrancy. Don't ever let anyone dim your light. Be bold and bright, create sparks, and radiate with abundance!

7. Harmony. Don't judge; be kind and forgiving, stay grounded, and embrace those who cross your path.

This book explores the waves of life, more accurately, my life—the ebb and flow of inspiration, love, tragedy, resilience, success, failure, hope, reason, growth, loss, and the pursuit of solace and peace. My journey through the sphere of business and life unfolded with unpredictable and often unrelenting waves. But throughout it all, invaluable experiences and profound insights helped me become a better person, a more connected leader, and a happier, more successful business owner.

It's incredible what the human spirit is capable of enduring, how we can indeed flourish amidst, and sometimes as a result of, the chaotic world of life interspersed with business, and how the transformative power of resilience and belief are essential in those who dare to dream to make those dreams a reality. For those who have experienced setbacks and failures, you can use the lessons learned from those experiences to do it better next time. And for those who seek to grow and evolve into their truest selves, all you need is inspiration and motivation—the spark that ignites your soul. I urge you to overcome your self-limitations, take risks, and defy the status quo that so many choose to live with.

But I'm not going to lie... Business is hard. Life is harder. There is no doubt about that. But if you work hard enough, you can succeed in both.

There are many aspects to this book that I am sharing with the hope that it will instil belief, self-love, and confidence in those who need it. I truly hope that you will find inner strength and trust in yourself to break through the barriers and hardship to make your way forward because your life depends on YOU...

CHAPTER 1

Through Young Eyes

I was born on 14 May 19 (let's just say a long time ago!) to my parents, David and Sandra Lewis. I'm the eldest child of three and the only girl. My two younger brothers, Daniel and Aaron, are two years apart consecutively. I was ten days overdue and born by Cesarean. My mum always said that I arrived late, and I was late from that moment on.

In my younger years, anyway. But I prefer to look at it as just having so much to squeeze into every moment that I didn't want to waste time sitting around waiting. Am I right!?

My name originated from an Alfred Hitchcock movie called *Marnie*, which was classified as a psychological thriller. My parents watched this when they were pregnant with me. In the movie, Marnie was played by Tippi Hedren, who was blonde-haired and blue-eyed. I'm not quite sure what resonated with them in this movie, as the storyline is about Marnie, (obviously) who had a very troubled upbringing. As an adult, she was a habitual thief and a liar who could not seem to stick to any job. And she went a little, ummm… let's just say weird when there was a thunderstorm or when she saw the colour red. Anyway, according to Mum, I was meant to be named Danielle. They had decided that if I was born with blonde hair and blue eyes, I would be Marnie, and if I was born with dark hair and dark eyes, I would be Danielle.

In those days, when women had a Caesarean, they were put under full anaesthesia, and then they had to go through the whole recovery process before seeing the baby. So, it was my dad who saw me first. I was born with a full head of thick black hair and green eyes, but he decided that I would be Marnie anyway. Needless to say, when Mum saw me, there was a little bit of confusion about whether she had the right baby. That was the beginning of my place in life as daddy's little girl. He got his way. I think he always wanted me to be Marnie, so he took the opportunity and ran with it. Oh, and my middle name is also for my dad. It's his initials, Del — David Ernest Lewis, D.E.L.

Growing up in the '70s and '80s meant life was all about being outdoors, camping, exploring nature, and playing in the dirt (or the creek as our location would have it). I grew up with a stay-at-home mum and a dad who loved speed - the fast, racing kind of speed, which meant that life was an adrenaline-filled adventure from the start.

We lived in a modest three-bedroom home in a cul-de-sac in Georges Hall, a small suburb in Southwestern Sydney. We were fortunate enough to have lots of "boys' toys," so being a tomboy was just a given for me. I never grew out of this, but I think I could be classified more as a girly tomboy these days.

My mum and dad loved water skiing, so we had a stream of speed boats over the years, and I was water skiing at 5 years old. We spent most school holidays and long weekends at Del Rio, a holiday park near Wisemans Ferry on the Hawkesbury River. We always had friends and family with us, and my dad taught literally dozens of people to ski. He was always in his element when he was helping people. His favourite boat was a 19-foot Connelly Craft speedboat, which was featured on the front cover of a boating magazine. He was so proud of that! It was called Hot Bubbles. I'll let you draw your own conclusion as to how he came up with that name.

From the age of 12, I have had my boat licence, and at that age, my dad was teaching me to drive his car—at rubbish tips, new housing sites, around our street, and anywhere else he thought we wouldn't get caught. I loved driving the boats and had a knack for manoeuvring them on and off the trailer, no matter what the current was like. My dad loved me doing this as it made his life so much easier—until we (I) forgot one time to put the bungs back into Dad's brand new jet boat, and while warming up in the middle of the river, I almost sank it. I was oblivious to him madly waving his arms and yelling at me to come back in. But I made it in. I had noticed the back end dropping under the water when I looked backward to find out why it was so sluggish. That was a very close call, but just one of the many times I managed to stress my poor dad out.

Dad bought my brothers go-karts, which they raced, but there was no way that I was going to be left out. I'm sure I must have been so annoying! No other girls were involved in this sport at the time, so I would always race against boys, which never concerned me. This love of racing turned into an opportunity in my late teens when I had the incredible experience of racing cars. My dad had a mate who owned an SLR Torana with a 454 Chevy Big Block engine which he was racing at Oran Park. Apparently, he was happy to let me be his co-driver. Well, at least I think he was - maybe he just owed my dad a favour. Either way, sitting on that grid line, the youngest by far and the only female at the wheel, was still one of the most exhilarating times of my life. I was just 17 or 18 when I started, and it's something that I wish I had continued doing. But it would have been a full-time commitment, and I had some big goals to fulfil by then. I've kept that passion alive with track days at Eastern Creek to satisfy that need for speed I inherited from my dad. Losing my licence AGAIN isn't an option.

And in regard to sport, all of the little girls I knew were playing netball. But I was far too rough for that - it turned out that basketball was a much better fit for me. I played representative basketball until my mid-teens, reaching the State and Australian National championships. This meant travelling all over the country to play, and I can thank my beautiful mum for driving me and flying with me to enable me to compete at this level. I played soccer as well—on the boys' team, of course—as there weren't any girls' soccer teams then.

We would also take our dirt bikes out on Sundays (my brothers had their own bikes; I shared my dad's), and we spent hours riding around in the bush. I have my road bike licence now and bought my first motorbike during what I like to refer to as my mid-life crisis, even though I don't think that stage has ever ended. I also had a BMX, which I spent hours on each week, riding around the neighbourhood and building jumps with the boys. I had one friend who also had a BMX, and she is, still to this day, one of my besties. We've remained friends since the age of 4, and she has been there for me through thick and thin. Life just wouldn't be the same without her! Although we're really polar opposites in almost everything, she's one of those friends that you hold close and never let go of. Trina - my grounding force always.

I still have a passion for driving and for beautiful cars, and it's one of the things I hope never to lose, contrary to what my genetics aim to do. But more about that later.

Our early childhood was very social; living in a cul-de-sac tends to bring people together. Our neighbours were all very close, and many are godparents to us and vice versa with my parents. Most of the out-of-school activities revolved around street cricket, pool volleyball, BMX biking, go-karts, dirt bikes, and hanging out in the drains that ran into the above-mentioned local creek. We often blocked off the street as we arranged many street parties for any occasion we could think of. There were always bonfires on a vacant block, the biggest on "Cracker night" for those of you old enough to remember when firecrackers were legal.

My dad was a go-getter who had a penchant for buying things and then selling them whenever someone made him a good offer. I guess you'd call him a born salesman. We always used to joke that we couldn't stand still for too long, or he would sell us too. Maybe that's where my inner sales warrior began to bloom, watching him negotiate his little side deals. However, I can say with certainty that I had no intention whatsoever of getting into sales then or any time remotely close to my childhood. But what I have discovered reflecting on those formative years is that I've had this innate determination and drive to try anything for as long as I can remember.

And a desire to keep up with the boys—I hated being left out of anything! And still do now.

I believe that our habits, beliefs, and behaviours become ingrained in us from early childhood just by watching and absorbing life around us. In fact, I read somewhere that it is up until we are 8 years old that our critical thinking and behavioural learning are the most prevalent and enduring. My life revolved around wanting to do everything my dad and my brothers did. I think I must have been a little hooked on the adrenaline rush because the little girl things my mum tried so hard to get me into just didn't work out for me. My mum would "encourage" me to do dancing, and I did for a while. I have to admit, my only recollection of this is of being onstage in a bumble bee outfit and yelling across the auditorium at her for eating my chips. I don't think the dance classes were my thing, so she gave up trying after a while.

My dad was a Civil Engineer by trade, but he had a passion for the simple life. He bought a furniture removal truck when we were young, and he was contracted to Grace Bros. as a removalist. The whole neighbourhood would use that truck as our cubby house; we spent hours playing in it. I loved nothing more than going to work with him, sitting in the middle of him and his offsider reading out the addresses and the furniture to be delivered. He, of course, would always double-check my advice after a wrong delivery or two (oops). He had an incredible memory for directions, and he was my version of a nav-man when I started driving (legally). I am ALWAYS getting lost. I clearly didn't inherit this part of him. I am so sure that I was born without that little inbuilt radar that we're supposed to have in our brains. You know, the "sense of direction"? Well, mine is missing. Seriously, spin me around three times and point me in the right direction, even on a drive that I have driven dozens of times, and I'll still go the wrong way. Oh well, we can't be good at EVERYTHING! It's just lucky that I love driving.

Dad's job was physically very hard on him, and some injuries forced him to look for a new career path. He was soon accepted for a position with Mercedes Benz Commercial, where he progressed to being the National General Manager, a huge accomplishment we were all very proud of. But this was where things started to get harder for our family. Part of Dad's job meant that he had to travel overseas for up to nine months of the year. This left Mum alone to take care of us three kids, and it caused trouble between them. I often heard the arguments on the phone, and I would spend many nights with a pillow over my head, trying to block it all out. Being very close to my dad and having spent so much time with him prior to this made it extremely difficult for me to adapt to him not being around all the time. Eventually, it was decided that he would look for another career opportunity due to the pressure it was putting on the family.

Dad arrived home one day and told Mum that he wanted to buy a truck yard. It was a small business operating in Fairy Meadow, an outer suburb of Wollongong. We were still living in Sydney, and Mum had concerns about the regular commute, but he was adamant that he would be able to do it. This was what he really had always wanted. His own business. So, Dad purchased that truck yard, and off he went, travelling down to Wollongong each day. He transformed that business into one that was known Nationally—a small truck yard in an industrial location, which ended up being the supplier for many of the businesses within the Steelworks as well as other transport businesses and independent truckers around the country.

I was still spending as much time as I could with Dad. I seemed to be "sick" a lot in those days so that I could go to work with him. I also spent every weekend and school holidays there too. I loved driving the trucks around the yard, answering phones, and helping with paperwork. I was learning so much, and I was obsessed with watching Dad's business grow. Dad was great at sales; he had the proverbial "can sell ice to an Eskimo" kind of ability. And he had no issue with thinking outside the square either. If somebody didn't have the money to pay for a truck, it was no problem! He would just ask them what else they had to trade. To give you an idea of how he worked, some of the things he traded for trucks over the years included a house, an emerald ring, lots of sports cars, including a bright yellow Convertible Porsche Boxster, and a boat, just to name a few (pretty cool and very innovative, huh!) This was definitely setting the groundwork for my future in business—doing whatever it takes to make it work.

While things were going well for him with work and the family finances were much stronger, things were still changing on the home front. I loved my mum very much, but like many teenage girls and their mums seem to go through, there was a lot of miscommunication and misunderstanding of each other. I was very confused about our relationship and couldn't understand why I always upset her. I know now that she had her own challenges, and her strict rules and lack of positive affirmation, affection, and trust were borne from a deep-rooted fear of not being able to protect me. She wanted to keep me safe above all else. But as a teenage girl, I mistook or had no understanding of this. I just thought that she didn't like me. In fact, if I'm being honest, I sometimes thought she hated me, which was absolutely not the case. She just didn't know how to show her feelings.

My timelines and recollection of the two years from here are quite blurred, so you'll have to forgive my vagueness. I also don't want to share too much private and personal information about my parents and their relationship, as this isn't the focus of this book. It's not my story to tell.

However, I believe sharing my reactions as a teenager to some of the events and their impact on me will help explain their lasting effects.

Mum and Dad separated when I was around 13-14 years old, and a lot of anger and emotion was involved. It wasn't an amicable split. For a period of time, we weren't allowed to see Dad. This, combined with the confrontations and other stuff that we were told or overheard, created a lot of uncertainty, which often goes along with this kind of thing. I felt like I was in the middle of a war zone.

To this day, I don't handle confrontation well. I do anything to avoid it. I am a people pleaser, so I like everybody to be happy, and I like to be surrounded by calm and positive energy. So, during this time, I had an all-encompassing and overwhelming feeling of failure in not being able to make everybody happy again. Life was an emotional roller coaster that I couldn't get off of. This triggered a decline in my mental well-being and my feeling of safety and security at home. I began to isolate myself. I became a loner and started having nightmares, mostly about wolves and devils with glowing red eyes hiding in cupboards and under benches in the house. I tried to run from them, but I couldn't move. I'd try to scream, but no sound would come out. I would wake up, literally paralyzed with fear. Too scared to sleep, I'd often try to keep myself awake by reading all night. This, in turn, affected my mood every day after. Everything around me was spiralling out of control, and I could not stop it.

My parents got back together after a while, but my inner turmoil and trust issues remained for a long time. Maybe it was a sense of fear that it would happen again—deep and unresolved blame—or possibly the raw emotion and anger that I didn't know how to cope with.

I don't actually know why it had such an impact, but it did. I started to act out with some pretty embarrassing and ugly behaviour, which I'm ashamed to admit to. I started sneaking out at night, drinking—I would sneak swigs of alcohol from my parent's bar regularly—and I was even filling my school drink bottle with spirits and drinking it at the bus stop, so I went to school drunk. I guess it helped to numb the thoughts in my head and slow down the nightmares.

I started skipping classes at school, then days, then weeks. I quit basketball, preferring to hang out in the drains behind the stadium. Yep, very classy stuff. I also started wearing makeup, a lot of it. This is significant because it became my mask over the years. It was almost like putting on makeup created a whole new persona for me – my security, my confidence, and my shield against the world. For years and years, I wouldn't go out without it.

There was one more point that may or may not have had some effect on my mental state during this time. It's the colour red. It was always my mum's favourite colour. But I'm a Taurean—a bull. Surely you know what they say about waving a red rag at a bull and the consequences of such action? Well, my entire room had been red—the cupboards, curtains, desk.

Mum did some research and found some information shown below. I'm sure that she was looking for reasons and solutions for my "nonconformity, antisocial and rebellious behaviour." Maybe she was right.

Our brains can perceive the beauty and nuances of colour, but colour can impact humans on deeper levels. Science is continually learning more about the ways colour affects people. Colour brings about several visceral responses. Here are half a dozen ways that colour can sway humans.

- *Emotions*
- *Energy level*
- *Libido*
- *Appetite*
- *Creativity*
- *Memory*

The connection between the zodiac and colour is vital. This part relates directly to the Taurus zodiac sign.

Red is a striking colour that elicits a response. In the case of Taurus, the colour can be overwhelming and irritating. Consider the fact that bulls are enraged by the colour red as a good indicator that the colour should not be on the palette.

Who knows whether it had any relevance to how I felt? Luckily for me (not at the time, though!) I got caught. As you can imagine, all hell broke loose at that point. There was talk of rehab or boarding school and lots and lots of tears (and yelling) from everyone. But the thing was, I didn't need any of that. All I needed was to know that I was safe, loved, and had peace and equilibrium in my life. My parents gave me an ultimatum and grounded me indefinitely. They tightened the strings so tightly that I was like a prisoner in my own home—no friends, no going anywhere after school, no freedom whatsoever. This in itself just made me feel more resentful, more misunderstood, and more isolated than I was already. I totally disconnected emotionally from my home life. Essentially, locking me up and being angry at me was justifying all of the things I was fighting against.

So, I ran away. Well, kind of. I have an aunt with whom I'm very close. In fact, she's more like a sister to me and has been there for me my whole life. I love her to bits, and I feel she is the reason I was able to turn my life around. I owe her everything. She was working in the city at the time. So, one night, I packed my bags, snuck out of the house (walking purposely through the flour my mum had sprinkled on the floor to catch me in the act or at least have evidence of my guilt), and got on a train. I disappeared. My aunt, of course, took me in and allowed me to spend some time with her. I could talk to her, and she would then communicate what I couldn't express at the time to my parents.

It's important to remember that I was already going through the hard teenage years of physical, emotional, mental, and social change, so there were more considerations than just what was happening in my family life. I think I was just overwhelmed with everything at that stage. Eventually, we came to a truce, and I went back home. And I changed rooms.

I take full responsibility for the decisions I made; I don't blame anyone else for my actions. Just so you know, this isn't a "poor me" story. I've never felt like a victim. Well, actually, once or twice, I think I could consider myself a victim, but we will get to that. When I was back home, I stopped thinking about myself for a moment and actually looked at things from my parents' perspective. I saw the fear, disappointment, and pain on their faces and knew that it was me inflicting that on them. I was devastated. I never wanted to hurt them, and that in itself was enough reason for me to pull myself out of the spiral I was in.

My mum and I had a really beautiful and loving relationship later in life. I think I needed to become an adult for her to understand that she could let go. She shared things with me that gave me a completely different perspective and a much deeper understanding of her and how and why she expressed emotion the way she did. It's just crazy how quickly and how easily we can slip into a negative and unhealthy trajectory, and I thank goodness that I was caught and that they took the steps they did to change things because life could have been very different for me otherwise.

From a very early age, I seemed to have developed a strong habit of taking responsibility for the happiness of others and bottling up my emotions to keep the peace. I wanted to prove my worthiness and make amends for whatever trouble I had caused. But with this came intense pressure, which I was putting on myself. I was aiming for self-perfection. I felt as though if I could achieve this, then there would be no need for people to be disappointed in me. I realise now that perfectionism comes from insecurity. It's a vicious cycle because you are forever trying to live up to an impossible standard and then feel like a failure when you can't achieve it. It has only taken me 40 years to recognise that there is no such thing as perfect. And the only person who expected anything like that of me was myself. So, all I really needed to do was to accept myself. Appreciate me, and forgive me. But as a teenager, the expectations that I was building for myself were fortifying.

You can likely tell that I was always a high achiever, trying to prove myself by being a girl caught up in a world of boys. But I think this may have been the most prolific time for me to develop the strongest desire to make people proud of me—never realising that they already were proud of me. Again, it took almost 40 years to recognise this and for me to learn that it wasn't what I ACTUALLY needed either. I was seeking pride in myself. I needed to be proud of ME.

Once I had my big epiphany about turning around my downfall, I turned my wayward attention toward getting my first job—in fact, I got two.

My first jobs at age 14 were as a checkout chick at our local supermarket, and on Thursday nights and Saturdays, I would work in a beauty salon on reception, stocking shelves and answering phones.

I wasn't worried about starting there and being open to learning and absorbing life along the way. All I knew was that I had to be good at everything I did, and I always had some deep understanding that the right opportunity would come to me when it was meant to. After all, it had happened for my dad, so it could happen for me, too.

As early as high school, when people would ask me what I wanted to be when I grew up, my reply was always the same.

"I want to own my own business."

"Doing what?" They'd inevitably ask.

"I don't know yet."

I guess that I was following my dad's footsteps by default.

My later teenage years were much better, although I still managed to push the boundaries. But I always got caught, and that in itself was a big life lesson for me. It didn't mean that I stopped doing things that I shouldn't have, but I did them with the knowledge that I would have some explaining to do at some point down the track. Touchè. Still what I live by now.

I'll finish off this chapter of my life by sharing one of my greatest learnings.

All of life's experiences happen for a reason. In time, you will look back and understand what that is. For me, while there were challenges, they also set the groundwork for my drive and tenacity that helped me so many times when it came to growing businesses. Never judge yourself too harshly when you do something you're not proud of. There isn't a single person on this planet who hasn't made a mistake or regretted something.

Life is never going to be perfect. But it's your life, so never forget that every day is a new day to change what you're doing if you are not happy.

CHAPTER 2

Building Blocks to Success

Finishing school was a blessing after almost being expelled in year nine for my drunken behaviour.

Once I finished my HSC (Higher School Certificate), I had a full-time job lined up for the next day. I was still 17, as I'd started school when I was only 4. I had travelled a bit with my family while growing up and found a real love for adventure and exploring new places—so I wanted more of that, too. I knew that I needed to earn decent money for this, so I decided to use this job as a stepping stone to fund my travels and get some workplace experience before deciding what I really wanted to do. I have always loved writing. So, journalism was at the top of my list, but at 17, I knew I had to experience more of life and explore several options before the right opportunity would come up for me. The business ownership dream was always in the background at this stage.

My first role started as a file clerk. Basically, that meant that I would get everybody's paperwork, file it away, make coffee, sometimes answer phones, and just run around and be what we used to call "the shit-kicker." I knew what I was in for, but there was no way that I was staying in that role for long. I managed to always get everything done quickly and efficiently, and then I would be at my supervisor's desk asking for more work. They started to pass over more, and after only a few months, I was promoted to creditors clerk.

Hmmm. That was not ideal, considering how much I hated maths, and it was certainly never my strong point. But while this role didn't excite me, I just went about it as outstandingly as possible, saving money and looking forward to the trip I was planning.

Finally, after about six months, it was time for me to go and book my tickets. I wanted to make sure I went on this trip before my career started to take off, as I knew there would be limited opportunities to be away for three to six months then.

My bestie, whom I mentioned earlier, and I decided that we would take a trip to Europe together, starting with a Contiki tour and then enjoying some time of exploration while staying with my aunt, who had relocated to England by this stage. We saved and planned for months, and the day before we were to buy the tickets, things changed in her world, and it was decided that it wasn't the right time for her to go on this trip.

Although I was devastated and initially thought that I should wait until she was ready, my parents encouraged me to continue on my own. That's a pretty daunting prospect for a 17-turning 18-year-old to consider, right?!

I was absolutely terrified at the prospect of travelling overseas by myself because, obviously, there were no mobile phones, social media, email, or any other method of keeping in contact at that time—besides letters and postcards or finding a payphone and having enough local cash to make a call—and praying they would be home to receive it. But of course, I decided to take a leap of faith and go for it.

I booked my tickets, and I took three months off work. Mum and Dad took me to the airport, and there was a mix-up with my booking, so my dad managed to get me upgraded to business class for the trip over (those negotiation skills came in handy once again!). Obviously, this made it much more exciting; I'm not going to lie! But I was still an absolute mess.

I remember getting on the plane in a tumult of tears (yes, the blubbering, snotty kind of tears) and sitting on the edge of my seat in business class, still considering doing a runner. As they were closing the doors, I started unbuckling my seatbelt but couldn't quite get it off in time. Luckily, a lovely flight attendant came up and asked me what I drank, which at the time was Tia Maria (don't judge me). So, he brought me out a large glass of straight Tia Maria to calm my emotions, or more specifically, to get me to stop crying. There was no attention available for crying babies on board that flight. The poor hosties were flat-out pacifying this supposedly grown woman, making a bigger ruckus than any baby was.

To make matters worse, my mum slipped an envelope into my handbag before boarding. I asked her what it was, and she told me not to read it until I got on the plane. I wish I still had that letter because it was a pivotal point in my relationship with my mum. She expressed a lot about the way she felt in that letter and explained a lot of things. I guess she was more like me than I ever thought. We can both write better than we can verbalise our emotions. While this was a very cathartic and beautiful moment, reading it made it all the harder to leave them for such a long time.

Now, there's no need to go into detail about the trip; I'm sure that you can draw your own conclusions about how things changed once I finally arrived. I mean… 18 years old, Contiki (aka PARTY) tour. Whatever you're thinking, we probably did. And more. It was certainly character-building, and besides the hangovers and the weight gain from all of the alcohol, the lessening of my previously held standards of hygiene, cleanliness, and diet—it brought me confidence, independence, and growth—yes, emotionally and mentally as well as in girth.

Going alone engaged my need to meet new people. When you do things alone, you're more likely to connect and build new friendships with those around you. You're almost forced into being upfront and open rather than sticking within your circle and, therefore, your comfort zone.

On the surface, people always say that I look like an extrovert. But I'm not. Anybody who knows me well will confirm that I am actually very shy and introverted, especially in social situations. In business, I am much more outgoing and confident. Wait, does that make me an introverted extrovert? Or an extroverted introvert?

Anyway, I am forever grateful to my parents for encouraging me to go on that trip because those memories will remain with me forever, and it confirmed a strength in me that I didn't know I had. It was also instrumental in building trust in myself to take that leap of faith in times when I don't think I can do something. I have very quickly learned in life that it's okay to be scared because it means you're about to do something really brave. It also means that you're about to learn something about yourself. Facing our biggest fears is super important for personal growth. You are proving to yourself that you CAN do it. Because what you CANNOT confront, you can never conquer. So, the fears that you don't face today will become your limitations tomorrow.

The trip also brought my mum and I closer. I spent a few days in Singapore for the last leg of my trip. When I got off the plane, bedraggled and absolutely exhausted, I walked out of that airport and saw my mum standing there. She had surprised me and turned up to spend the last few days with me. This was such an incredible moment and something really special for us to have done together. However, there was the fact that she couldn't believe that I only washed my clothes every so often and would turn my undies inside out to get another wear out of them (so gross, I know!) But that's what we were degraded to on those tours. If you've ever done one, you'll understand! But if you have and never did that, don't tell me. I prefer to live with my belief that is how everybody travels on Contiki tours. My mum was one who washed every single day, twice a day so that she could separate the lights and darks, and she ironed everything! That includes underwear, towels, sheets, and hankies. So, she had no understanding of how that could be possible. She also loved to shop (which I hate). So, I paid my penance by being dragged around for the next three days to look at every shop in Singapore. I'm sure we didn't miss one.

Side note: I know she would be horrified today to know I still don't own an iron. And I still hate shopping. But I do wash my clothes after each wear. I promise.

Once I got back to work, I had no money left, and I knew it was time to start building my career. I proceeded to work harder than ever, and eventually, I caught the attention of the accountant who was working in the head office. He offered me a job as an assistant accountant alongside him. More proof that it doesn't matter where you start. Stand out, and you'll be noticed. I was still only 18, so this was a really big promotion for me and one that I was very grateful for. But it was also my first big sliding door moment. You see, I didn't want to be an accountant. I hated maths, remember? I wanted to write, to be creative. But then again, I had to consider the bigger picture. Maybe doing accounting wouldn't be such a bad thing for when I have my own business. Surely, it would come in handy. Yes, so I accepted the new position and decided to see where this path was going to lead me.

I had to do an Associate Diploma in Accounting and struggled through some of it, mainly due to boredom (sorry to all you accountants out there). I stuck with it because I knew that, if nothing else, this opportunity had come to me for a reason. I did nine hours a week at my course plus the study and assignments time while working full time in my new job. I was busy!

One morning, I woke up and was getting ready for work and realised how quiet the house was. I went upstairs and couldn't find my parents, and both of my brothers were still asleep. At that moment, the phone rang, and I answered to hear my mum on the other end. She told me that my dad was in hospital, and they suspected he had had a heart attack. My dad was only in his early 40s at the time, and as I'm sure you will have noticed from my previous chapter, he was a huge part of my life. I was beside myself with worry. I can't even begin to explain the emotions that were running through my body at that time. I got in the car and drove straight to the hospital, somehow avoiding a speeding fine. I walked into the hospital and saw my dad sitting in a bed, covered in wires and monitors and with an oxygen mask covering his face. But I could still see the smile in his eyes. I will never forget that look; he was telling me he was okay, that he loved me, and that he wasn't ready to leave— without the need for words. The eyes have the capacity to express so much.

My dad spent about a week in hospital and underwent surgery after he had another heart attack while in there. He was very fortunate that my mum recognised the signs when she did, as he did not want to go to hospital, and he kept putting the symptoms down to other things. This occurrence rocked our family in a really big way, and my mum decided that it was not healthy for my dad to be travelling down to Wollongong every day, as the business had grown, and he was working very long hours and often up to 7 days a week. They decided to relocate and bought an apartment in Wollongong for the interim so that he would have somewhere to stay during the week until they had purchased a new family home and sold ours. This was the next sliding door moment in my life as I was at a crossroads as to whether to move with them or remain in Sydney and further my career in accounting.

During the time it took to sell the house, I remained in my job and continued my studies. Once my parents purchased a home in Kiama, on the New South Wales South Coast, which was even further away than Wollongong, I knew that eventually I would have to make a decision.

Initially, I stayed with my grandma for a few nights a week and commuted the other two between Kiama and Sydney. As time went on, I found myself spending more time in Kiama. I rescued a horse from a property that had gone into receivership, and I was spending a lot of time bringing her back to health. She was in incredibly poor condition, so she needed to be stabled and hand-fed two to three times a day. I had also fallen for somebody who would eventually be the father to my children and my husband, so as with all new and flourishing relationships, spending nights away in Sydney wasn't ideal.

The commute was a minimum of 4 and up to 6 hours round-trip each day, depending on the traffic, so add that to my 10-hour workdays and my 9 hours in class each week, as well as looking after my horse and it was making for a very draining schedule on my part. However, my job was going really well, and I flew all over Australia every three months to do the quarterly accounts for all of the subsidiary offices we had in each state - I loved that aspect of my job.

By now, I was 21 years old, and it was an opportunity not often given to somebody of my age. But I was also very tired, and I could see my life was rolling out in a different direction—I wanted to be closer to my family and live the life that was opening up for me in Kiama. I spoke to my employers, who were supportive but sad that I was thinking of leaving. They offered me significant incentives to stay. But I had made up my mind, and while we're all being honest here, accounting in itself was still not exciting to me. So, again, I took a leap of faith, this time into the unknown, and I left my job to relocate permanently to the South Coast.

Seeing as I was now unemployed, my boyfriend and I decided that we would take the opportunity to travel around Australia for a few months. Oh, and I had also kind of just lost my driver's licence for three months. I'm sure you can guess why. Perfect timing to get out of the state! We had a super cool, bright yellow Toyota Coaster bus that had been converted into a campervan. We had the most incredible time on this trip. We went to many out-of-the-way places, found some incredible little towns, and camped on the sand of deserted beaches and beautiful, vibrant blue lakes. We swam with dolphins and dodged too many crocodiles for my liking. But living together 24/7 wasn't easy. When we returned, we separated for a while. We just needed some space. But I also needed time to heal.

During this trip, I developed an eating disorder. Knowing what I know now about the usual causes, I believe it was a coping mechanism for situations in which I wasn't in control of my life. It was also a result of unresolved emotional issues, low self-esteem, and insecurity. However, it was also triggered by a seemingly innocuous comment from someone I loved very much. That comment made me feel as though I needed to be skinny, as though I wasn't good enough. A person's choice of words can have a profound impact, especially if someone already struggles with self-esteem. If I were in the place I am now, I would've laughed it off. But, unfortunately, I was in a very sensitive place then. I took that comment to heart because I wanted to be perfect for that person. It made me feel as though I wasn't meeting that expectation. Again, there's no blame to be placed on anyone else. I chose to let it affect me. I didn't seek clarification, but instead, I formed my own interpretation and narrative around it.

It started out more as Anorexia on the trip but developed into Bulimia once I was back, and there was more pressure to eat from those around me trying to help. I was literally skin and bones by the time we returned. There were many combined factors for this eating disorder to have manifested, and over the years, recurrences have been triggered by periods of acute stress and grief. I think it became a form of self-punishment. When things around me spiralled out of control or when I blamed myself for certain situations, I would relapse. Eating disorders are often caused more by psychological issues than by weight-related issues. But they tend to intertwine.

This is, obviously, a difficult subject for me. Many people reading this, who know me, will be shocked to learn about this part of my life. I don't talk about it. I'm ashamed of it, and I've been a prisoner to it for many years. But I want to talk about it because I am being authentic. This is me—raw and uncensored.

I'm sharing the bad with the good in the hope that if others have dealt with or are dealing with an eating disorder, you may find strength and motivation to fight back, knowing that you are not alone. It is a lot more common in young women than people think. It took me many years, on and off, as my life went up and down to get on top of it. I didn't ask for help when I should have, so gaining control of it has been a lifelong fight. Most people just don't understand it, which is another reason most sufferers don't share it with others who may be able to help them. Drugs, alcohol, and food abuse. These are all methods people use to cover up or numb pain, or they use them as self-punishment. They are all addictive, and they can all do terrible things to your body.

Through trial and error, persistence, and a lot of willpower, I've learnt many other ways to manage stress, trauma, anxiety, misfortune, loss, grief, and any other kind of hardship that has also triggered a relapse in the past. Sometimes, we're tested not to show our weaknesses but to discover our strengths. I have had health issues as a result of this, but I am somehow fortunate that the damage I've done to my body has not been permanent. I know that I have to keep fit, eat well, and do plenty of mindfulness and self/care practice. I also have to manage my responses and reactions to situations, which I believe play a big part in the way that I deal with pressure.

I thought I'd share some of my newly formed habits to help me avoid potentially stressful situations and assist me in staying within my own space, authentic to what I believe and want, and aligned with my goals and aspirations in my personal life and business life.

1. If it doesn't feel right, don't do it, regardless of who I offend.
2. Speak my truth, not what I believe will make others happy.
3. Try not to be a people pleaser, but please people with my happiness and voice.
4. Trust my instincts and act accordingly rather than doing what others want me to do.

5. Stop the negative self-talk. I consciously change any narrative in my head that isn't positive and encouraging.

6. Never give up on my dreams. I keep reminding myself that I can do anything.

7. Always have kindness in my heart and intentions towards others. This stops judgement and unwarranted opinions—even if others are judging me.

8. Let go of what I can't control and focus on what I can. Sometimes that is my reaction to a situation, or it is what is happening around me.

9. Remove myself from drama and negative people and situations. This happens naturally when you embrace the power of positivity and self-confidence.

10. And the big one for me is learning to say no. It's so much harder to say no than yes, and as a self-proclaimed people-pleaser, this one is tough!

Prior to setting these boundaries for myself, I would allow my "people-pleasing" to put everyone else first. Which resulted in me living with regret for the things I didn't say, agreeing to things I really didn't want to do, being stuck in situations and promises that I couldn't commit to, guilt that I let them down, anxiety over not being authentic and living my own way and suffocation from always trying to live up to the expectations I set for myself within other people's parameters.

And then there is the exercise and relaxation, which has always been my biggest satiation. I try to do the following daily.

- *Meditation*: Even if it's only 15 minutes a day.

- *Grounding*: Taking my shoes off and walking on sand or the grass, feeling the sensation under my feet.

- *Journaling*: Writing down my feelings helps me understand my emotions when something is not going how I want. I then write down all the things that are going right.

- *Gratitude*: I make a note of three things every day that I am grateful for.

- *Talking about it*: I find someone I trust and just tell them what's happening. I don't want them to try to fix it or give advice; mostly, it's just getting it out.

- *Being kind to myself*: I've learnt to take the pressure off when it gets too much and allow myself to just be. Releasing my self expectations.

- *Don't overthink*: Trusting my gut instinct and not over-complicating everything.

Overthinking is the big one for me here. I'm a worrier. An inward thinker. I create scenarios in my mind that weren't even there to begin with. I know that stressing about something won't change the outcome, no matter how many ways I look at it. And trying to find reason and rationale for situations that have no reason or rationale is just wasted energy. So, I make a conscious effort these days to notice when I'm starting to stress, work out what the cause is, and focus on processing it so that I can then let it go.

For those who have someone in their lives suffering from an eating disorder, I wanted to share a little insight into how you may best support them. Most people have no understanding of it, and nor should you. It's far more complex than anyone would think. But it's important to note that I'm not a therapist, and this is not meant to be professional advice. It's purely based on my own experience. Often, fear causes extreme reactions. So when we see someone that we love who is self-harming, it's a natural reaction to be angry. But please try not to be angry, and don't judge, shame, or guilt them.

And it's not usually beneficial trying to force them to stop or to eat or not eat, whichever the case may be.

This is an illness, and we wouldn't do that to someone fighting a physical illness or disease.

Just do your best to stay calm and supportive, love them harder than ever, but do not suffocate them with attention and supervision as it just builds resentment and can push them deeper into their pain and away from you. And they will just look for better ways to hide it. The fact of them just knowing that you know is enough. It's an embarrassing and shameful disorder for the person suffering, and it's usually well hidden from everyone. So gently explaining that you are aware will make them think twice about what they are doing and be more conscious of their actions around you. Which is a big step in healing. It's definitely a one-step-at-a-time process.

Let them know how much you care and tell them that you are there for support whenever they need you.

Be their safety, and provide a space where they can talk about it without judgement or you trying to fix anything. Just listen and accept where they're at. Be the buoy they can hold on to when the swell gets too much. A place they can breathe. And always shine a light, be the beacon of hope, so they know where to head towards when they're ready to start swimming again. That is the best thing that you can do.

And it's not wise to tell them that they need professional help. Instead, ask them if they want professional help. If and when they come to that realisation themselves, all you have to do is be there throughout the process and let them know you will be involved as little or as much as they want you to be.

Deep breath. Time to move on.

Once I was well enough, I went looking for work. I called a couple of employment agencies, and then I basically went and knocked on doors. One of those doors was a local car dealership, one of the biggest in the area. They didn't need an accountant at the time, but they had recently sold another dealership and offered to pay me as a contractor to finalise the accounts and wind up the company. This was perfect for me. It was good money, and I could work my own hours. So, I started on this and finalised it within the required scope. I was then offered a job at the dealership as an assistant accountant. Sometimes, you need to take a little step backward in order to move forward. Be prepared to prove yourself before expecting something to be given to you.

After about a year there, I received a call from the recruitment agency asking whether I was still open to an opportunity. I knew that accounting wasn't where I was meant to be ultimately in my career, so I told them that I would love to hear more about the role.

I went in to meet the person who was looking to fill the role, and he was a local property developer. He had recently started his business and was looking for somebody to fill the role of PA (Personal Assistant) and be able to do the accounts and other day-to-day activities as needed. After sitting and chatting for close to an hour, he offered me the job on the spot. Those sliding door moments again. This is how I got into the real estate industry.

I started working with him a couple of weeks later and enrolled in the Property Licensing course. I loved this course and breezed through the modules with high marks. I was responsible for assisting on a number of activities, including dealing with councils for approvals on development sites, liaising with architects, lodging development applications and building applications, sourcing and doing feasibility studies on opportunistic sites, and helping with proposals to bring in joint venture partners. I found this role so much more exciting. Although I had never thought about a career in the real estate industry, it was vastly different from what I had done, and I found it extremely interesting. It also gave me a lot of insight and knowledge about off-the-plan sales in both subdivisions and apartment complexes. This has proven to be invaluable over the years in dealings with developers on their projects.

One of the biggest projects that I assisted on was Shell Cove, which is a new suburb in the Shellharbour local government area, and it is built around what is now a new harbour and marina. There are thousands of house blocks, and the project has been in development and sale for almost 30 years now.

This period of time was an incredibly happy time for me. I got engaged (yes, my boyfriend and I reunited), bought my first home at 22, got married at 24, sold and bought a bigger home at 25, and fell pregnant with my first daughter when I was 27. Life was incredible.

I worked in this role and other contract roles with associated excavation and building companies for five years before I was again headhunted to join a local Kiama real estate agency. I went into the real estate office and I was at the front desk when the office manager walked out. He recognised me; he was the head TAFE teacher who I had done my property licensing course with. He asked me what I was doing for work. An hour later, he called me and asked whether I would be interested in meeting him and the owner of the business for a coffee the next day, which I did.

Cue the next sliding door moment… I had never worked in residential sales, or any sales for that matter. Another leap of faith? You betcha! I would be close to home, which was perfect, as I had recently had my first daughter, my beautiful Carla. My daughter brought out a love in me that I never dreamed could ever exist. The less travel I had to do, the more time I could be with her. And being open to possibilities from any angle—that's what we're meant to be doing, right? But sales? Hmmm. Okay, let's see how this goes. (Dad! I think I'm going to need you!)

So, of course, I jumped at the opportunity. Obviously, this one was most definitely meant to be. These synchronicities don't just happen. By this stage, I was very much learning to trust my instincts and look for the paths opening up and then heading towards what felt right. Taking a leap of faith seems to have become a pattern for me, and so far, it has worked out the way I felt it was meant to. I didn't see any reason why this would be any different. And so, at 27 years of age, as a new mum, I embarked on what was to become the most influential journey of my life.

When you stop looking back, trying to make sense of what has been, and cease trying to predict the future by making assumptions about the unknown, you'll see and feel every moment as it happens, and you won't miss any detail or opportunity for growth and change.

And when everything falls into place, you'll see the bigger picture and know that everything happened for a reason, and it will all make perfect sense. Trust your journey and have faith in your destiny by relinquishing expectations of what SHOULD be and allowing what COULD be to take its place.

CHAPTER 3

Embracing Opportunity

So, the real estate sales agent life began. I started my new job in the middle of winter, in a market cycle that commonly saw properties sit on the market for years. I had absolutely no idea what I was doing, and the day that I started, it was blowing a gale, absolutely pouring rain, and it had been doing so for the past week.

My manager had gone on holiday, and when I arrived at the office, I had a phone and a reverse phone book sitting on my desk. In case you've forgotten, in those days (we're talking 1998), we didn't have mobile phones, we didn't have computers, we didn't have any kind of navigational equipment, we didn't have email, and we didn't have the Internet, I don't think. *Sounds like fun, huh!?*

I was told to make some calls to get appraisals.

"What do I say?" I asked.

"Whatever you have to."

Great. So, I did what I was told. I only had one unsavoury response that first week. "Don't you have anything better to do? I'll come to you if I want to sell my home!" Bang!

"Uhhh no, not really. It's pouring," I muttered into the dial tone as I also hung up. The joys of cold calling.

Things quickly got better as I managed to pick up around 13 leads across the two weeks my manager was gone. My first appraisal ended up being a waterfront property. We didn't get the listing, but it was an incredible experience, and I learnt a lot more from NOT being successful in that first listing presentation. But it turned out I was a better salesperson than I had ever thought possible, which is interesting because I have never been your stereotypical salesperson.

My approach has always been about building connections. There were a lot of older traditional real estate agents in town and only one other female who was about to retire when I started, and they had a very different approach to me. To them, I was just some "youngster" who came in out of nowhere and didn't know anything, but I was full of energy, excitement, enthusiasm, and curiosity, and I had a real desire to make it work, all of which I believe surpasses experience a lot of the time. It shows your commitment to proving yourself and your willingness to work hard, not make excuses, and get the best result.

I think I was successful right from the very start because I had no idea what was meant to happen or how I was meant to do things. In those days, the real estate industry was quite different and certainly more male-dominated. I was just genuinely enjoying helping people, and my focus on client experience and communication stood out. I was also being very proactive in getting properties sold at a time when many other properties were still not selling.

In sales and business in general, I believe that the most important and influential thing that you can do is to bring people into the conversation and decision-making process rather than telling them what they should do. I always ask questions because that's the only way to find out exactly what the most important thing is to them and what information they actually want from you. Making everything about my clients to ensure that their expectations come first and foremost has always been my priority and something that many past clients relate back to me to this day.

As my career really started to take off, I fell pregnant with my second beautiful daughter, India. Again, that immeasurable love burned within me, and I found it so hard to leave my girls to go to work. But, I was very fortunate to have a close family network who helped with caring for my daughters. Without them, I'd never have been able to do what I have done. I am forever grateful.

Just after India was born, the franchisor who owned the agency in which I was working asked to have a meeting with me. We had spoken previously about business, and on my dad's advice, I mentioned that I would love to own a business someday and that I would be interested in buying in if he ever wanted to sell. But I had anticipated this to be quite a ways down the track. However, during this meeting, he offered me a 50 percent partnership in the business. I was blown away. Although I had brought it up previously, I certainly didn't think it would happen, especially so soon. It was an incredibly surreal moment for me. *Was my dream really coming true this early in my life and career?* The answer was yes. So many questions raced through my mind, but I almost screamed, "YES!" at him before I could overthink it or risk him changing his mind.

I was so excited that I didn't even stop to think about how I would get the money, how much I would need, or how I would manage a business with two very young daughters. My second daughter was only a few months old at the time. The truth is, I could have found many reasons why the timing was not right or to support the idea that I wasn't ready. But I knew that I would work all of that out. I wanted this and would do anything I had to do to make it work. Undoubtedly, I dived into this business headfirst without really thinking it all through. But then again, spontaneity is my middle name. (Well, not really, but it should be.)

The reality was that I had no business experience; I didn't have much real estate experience at that time, either. All of the staff were well and truly older than me and had many more years in the industry. I started to think, *Oh shittttt!* But then I quickly realised that none of that scared me. And it certainly wasn't going to stop me!

This just illustrates that there is never any harm in asking a question or planting a seed that could change your life and provide you with an opportunity that you may never have had otherwise.

I'll never forget going in to see our bank manager to ask him for a loan. We obviously had a mortgage; we were on our second home by then. Luckily, we had equity in it, so we were able to get a line of credit against our property.

While we were sitting in front of him discussing the business purchase, I remember him leaning over the desk, looking me directly in the eye, and asking me. "What is your plan B?" I must've looked quite confused because then he added, "If this doesn't work out, what will you do then?" I truly had not even thought about a plan B, and that is what I told him. It had never crossed my mind that this wouldn't work out. I am not sure whether it was because it had been something I had wanted for so long or it was because I just had so much faith and belief in this being the next stage of my journey— it just felt RIGHT. I knew that if I put in the work, I would make it successful. So I told my bank manager it would work because I would make it work. Hard work and long hours have never been an issue for me.

There was another agency in town closing at the same time, and they had a rent roll (property management portfolio) that they wanted to sell. We decided that the optimal way for me to buy into the business would be to purchase their rent roll and combine it with the existing business, which was of equal value. That's essentially what gave me my 50 percent share in the business.

Generally, when you purchase an existing business, and you come into that fresh, it is easier to demonstrate your leadership skills as the people working there have no knowledge of your background. I entered this business as a trainee, and in less than 18 months, I was the boss. This definitely took some adjusting for everybody, including me. It was a challenging time in switching roles and learning how to be an effective leader. The manager stayed on for the first year, which provided a great transition into me taking over the leadership reins once everybody had adjusted a little more and I had taken more notice of the way things were operating.

Once we had gotten through the first year, I decided I wanted full control over the business, so I offered to buy my business partner out and become the sole director and principal. I set up a company, which I named after my daughters. "Carlindi" was established in 2000 and became the entity for my 100 percent purchase of the business.

Back to the bank manager I went to ask for another line of credit. Maybe he had a little more faith in me by this time because it didn't seem to be as hard as it was at that first meeting. Plus, there was the fact that I had drastically increased the profitability of the business over that year—I'm sure that helped as well.

The following year, which was my first year as the sole owner, the profitability of the business jumped up over 400 percent, and we ended up having equal top market share in the area. I was recruiting new people, and we were working on building the rent roll and increasing our sales income.

When it came to my relationship with the team who had been there before me, it was an ongoing process to develop trust and respect. By the time we were into the second year, it was quite obvious to everybody that the business was thriving under my leadership, which meant more opportunities for everybody. Once the manager decided to move on, it was all on me, so there were several things that I worked on implementing and focused on to build rapport with my team moving forward.

Here are a few things that were instrumental in my first few years as a young business owner, taking over an existing team.

1. *Demonstrating competence*: Showing the team that I could handle the responsibilities of my role as business owner and salesperson. I read books on leadership (and asked my dad a million questions) and made sure that I was as well-prepared as I could be.

2. *Being open to learning*: It's important to recognise that we can learn from the experiences and wisdom of older team members. Showing a genuine interest in their knowledge and expertise and being open to their suggestions and advice was critical in building an alliance with them. It also showed humility and a willingness to grow and develop my skills.

3. *Communicating effectively*: Developing strong communication skills to clearly convey my thoughts, ideas, and expectations was key to building respect while actively listening to team members and valuing their input.

4. *Encouraging communication*: This created a supportive environment.

5. *Leading by example*: Setting a positive example through actions, work ethic, and results. Being accountable and always there to support their growth and success. Your team will only respect and trust you if they see you embody the qualities you expect from them.

6. *Building rapport*: Investing time and effort into building personal connections with team members is so valuable. Getting to know

them individually, understanding their strengths and what they want to achieve, and supporting their weaknesses to turn them into avenues of growth. This will show them that you care about their well-being and generate trust and loyalty.

7. *Seeking input through inclusivity*: Involving the team in decision-making processes whenever possible, considering their perspectives, and valuing their contributions shows that you respect their expertise and opinions, which increases trust and engagement. Inclusivity like this is something I have invested in every business.

8. *Adapt and be open*: Being willing to embrace new ideas, approaches, and ways of doing things helps to avoid being dismissive of different perspectives. I love collaborating and encouraging innovation, allowing team members to contribute their creativity to my business.

9. *Conflict resolution*: Conflicts may arise in any team, regardless of age differences. As a leader, addressing conflicts promptly and professionally builds a culture of respect and encourages constructive dialogue to resolve issues. Show fairness and impartiality when there is a need to mediate conflicts with empathy and understanding of all parties involved.

10. *Recognition and appreciation*: I've never had an "I'm the boss, you work for me" mentality. I am and always will be part of the team. So, for me, celebrating the achievements and successes of all team members is part of developing a great culture. Acknowledging their efforts with praise and meaningful recognition enhances a motivational work environment.

11. *Empathy and compassion*: Earning respect and trust takes time, especially when leading an older team. I am patient with the process and demonstrate empathy toward any challenges my team members

may face by showing understanding and support. I recognise that I can't just come in and demand respect—I have to earn it.

These first years as a business owner were amazing for me. I learned so much about myself, the financial aspect of business, and how to lead and manage a team while still growing my income as a sales agent and keeping the balance in my home life… sort of.

My dream was finally a reality. But with reality comes real-life consequences. In a dream, you can make it as perfect as you can imagine it to be. Once it's real, it's never so perfect. No matter how much experience you have as a leader, there will be challenging moments.

And trying to keep things together in your personal life alongside your business life is not always easy either.

CHAPTER 4

The Walls Come Tumbling Down

Remember my waves analogy at the beginning of this book? Well, this is where the waves really began to gain momentum. This period of my life was way tougher than I could ever have imagined it could be. Earlier, I said everyone makes mistakes. Well, some of the mistakes I made in this chapter were colossal. It all started when my daughters were just 3 and 5 years old. My husband and I separated and ultimately divorced. It was an emotional and gut-wrenching time for everyone involved, and my sole focus, as was my husband's, was maintaining as much normality, love, and support for our daughters as we possibly could. No divorce is easy, but as adults and parents, our decisions (as dumb, stupid, wrong, or right as they may be) should not affect our children's feelings of love and security. They're just the unwilling victims in these situations. I learned how important this is firsthand as a child.

The details in this part of my life are personal, and I don't feel they are relevant to this book.

But suffice it to say that with maturity, personal growth, a LOT of soul searching, and the advantage of hindsight, there are many things that I would change. I'm sure that everyone has regrets in life, but it's impossible to change the decisions that were made. This year involved a lot of hurt as my life seemed to spiral out of my control once again. I was still very determined to build the best life that I could for my daughters, and at this stage, I felt capable of running the business and caring for them.

By the time we entered 2004, I had 12 staff, and we were easily one of the biggest agencies in the area. But with so much happening in my personal life, I decided it was time for me to sell this business and spend more time with my daughters while they were so young.

At certain times in life, your heart will take you in a different direction than your previously planned out path. But there are many different routes you can take to reach the same destination. Even if the detour you're taking turns out to be a dirt track full of potholes and seemingly insurmountable mountains... Like the one I found myself on.

I approached the franchisor to advise of my decision to sell the business, and then I approached another agency owner who had just opened up in the area. I had a number of conversations with them about purchasing my business and rent roll. Over time, we came to an agreement, and we proceeded to formalise the details of the business sale and have Contracts drawn up. I sought advice from my solicitor and my accountant regarding selling the business because I still had six months left on my franchise agreement. There is a clause in these agreements stating that you can sell prior to the end of the fixed term. However, you have to pay an average of your franchise fees for the remaining term of the agreement, which I was prepared to do.

Probably mistake number 1—I should have just waited it out. But I was acting on impulse and emotion rather than common sense, so at this point, I think that I made some critical errors in my decision-making and my judgement. I had obviously never been involved in a business sale before, nor had I been involved with a franchise until this time. Nobody in my sphere of influence had either.

The purchasers and I agreed on a price, and we then proceeded to exchange contracts. One of their criteria for the sale was that I did not disclose any information to my staff about the sale or discuss it with anybody else until it was completed. The sale had to remain strictly confidential. I had a very close relationship with my team, and I knew how much they trusted me as their leader and friend. So this didn't sit well with me and didn't feel right. In addition, by the time we had negotiated the sale's final details and were ready to exchange, it was very close to Christmas, which added to the overall weight on my conscience for keeping this decision from them.

I didn't go with my instincts on this, I went with what had been requested by the purchaser of the business out of respect for them and also knowing how important this was for my family that the sale went through. The purchaser already had a team in place, and I am sure that if they were able to do so, they would have kept my team. I wasn't aware of exactly what was going to happen in this regard until contracts were exchanged. The purchasers were well within their rights to make this decision, but I felt responsible for my team losing their jobs. I have absolutely no ill feelings toward the purchaser, as they were absolutely protecting their assets. When you sell a rent roll, the onus is on the seller to transfer over all managements to the buyer, which has to be done manually. This is a critical period of time between exchange and settlement where anyone with knowledge of the sale could use the information to contact owners and take managements before we had any chance to transfer their agreements to the new business owners, so confidentiality generally gives the best security,

But of course, this came back to bite me—massively. I could say the universe was conspiring against me, but I believe it's the opposite. It's keeping me honest and teaching me to assert myself and trust my instincts.

My accountant sent me a letter confirming the details of the sale but didn't mark it private and confidential. So it was opened by one of my team, with the rest of the mail, and subsequently, everybody in the office knew what was happening before I could discuss why I had made this decision and the reasons behind it. It was a horrible way for my team, which I appreciated very much, to find out about the sale, and I totally understand their anger and disappointment. Although I had every right to sell my business and make decisions that were in the best interests of the purchaser, myself, and my daughters, it could have been handled better. I had no reason not to trust them.

When I got back into the office that day, I was bombarded by my team. Obviously, they were very upset and very angry.

Sometimes, it's not the decisions we make that are the problem. It's how we communicate and implement those decisions that cause the problem. Although I tried to explain everything to them, there was definitely not the understanding I had hoped for. Being between a rock and a hard place didn't help me, which is okay, and I am not in any way judging their reaction. In the same situation, I may have felt the same way. Most of them have not spoken to me since, which is not a comfortable place to be in for a people pleaser. Of course, I took it all on my shoulders, which added to an already difficult decision in selling the business in the first place.

My dad told me something during these difficult times of estrangement from so many people which is becoming so much more important and powerful the older I get. He said, "What people say & think about you is none of your business. We cannot control other people's opinions or thoughts, so no matter what you do, say, or be—it's unlikely to change anything." And why should you try to change their minds? Allow them to think what they want. Because what other people think can only affect you if you let it. If you let the judgement of others stop you from being you... Then you're no longer you. If you live to please others and go through life trying to make everyone else happy, you'll never be happy. He said, "Hold your head high. You know you're a good person and you are worthy of self-love and self-pride and that's all that really matters." We're not here to please everyone, and the sooner we let go of that need for the wrong people to love us, the sooner we notice and appreciate just how much the right people love us.

But things would only get worse for me. The real pain point in the sale of this business came from the franchisor.

During the last year, I was with the local franchise, they lost many offices to a rival franchise group. This group was expanding into the area, and they made contact a year earlier to see whether our group would be interested in rebranding as a whole.

After a meeting between the franchisor and us as the franchisees, we decided that it was a good opportunity to explore new options and take advantage of the training and other support this larger group could provide us. They offered a 12-month affiliation to see how it would work between the two franchise groups, so we worked together, co-branding and sharing information for that year. Once that was done, our franchisor decided not to proceed with the takeover and rebrand for unknown reasons. He had every right to make this decision, but what ended up happening was that each time one of our offices came to the end of their franchise agreement, they decided to rebrand to the other franchise.

Unfortunately for me, the buyer of my business was also part of that rival franchise, and so I became the final straw.

Within days of my team finding out about the sale, I was issued with a Summons to appear in the Supreme Court of New South Wales, along with documents from the court stating that I was being sued for damages to the sum of $1 million. There was also an injunction placed on me, preventing me from working for the purchaser. Not only did this stop me from working completely, as part of the business contract of sale stated that I had to commit to a two-year contract with them (which meant that I couldn't work for any other agency), but it also meant that I could not contact any of the clients to transfer managements over, as was also my obligation in the contract of sale— I was effectively bound and gagged.

$1 million was a lot of money in 2005, as it still is today, and a substantial amount more than I was selling the business for. At this point, the purchasers and I decided that we needed to settle straight away so they could get in and take control of the business while the court case went ahead. For this reason, as well as details of the sale then being public knowledge, we lost a lot of managements in the takeover. Rent roll sales in those days were negotiated at a set dollar amount based upon the last 12 months of income, multiplied by an agreed market price denominator. A retention amount, being a percentage of the total sale value, was held aside for any managements lost during the sale period.

These days, you work out the value in the same way, but you only pay for what you receive by way of transfers on an agreed progressive monthly settlement basis. So, there is far less risk to the purchaser.

This affected the purchasers greatly and meant that I lost my retainer, a substantial amount out of our negotiated sale price for the business.

I feel genuinely remorseful and sorry for the purchasers, who were just trying to do the right thing for their new business and for me. They were also included in the proceedings, with a claim being made against them for damages as well. Through no fault of their own, they, too, were dragged through months of court proceedings.

At the time all of this was happening, my parents were on holidays in Europe. I don't think I have ever felt so overwhelmed and helpless in my life. I literally didn't know where to start. *How do I fight this? What are my options? Who do I get to act on my behalf?* So many things that I had absolutely no idea how to manage at the time.

I was not given much notice for the initial court hearing; I had to be in court within 24 to 48 hours of the summons being issued. That meant finding people to look after my daughters and going to court without anybody to support me and help me digest what was happening.

Until my other absolutely amazing and supportive bestie came to my rescue. Thank God for Ali! She spent days holding my hand and letting me cry on her shoulder during this entire process, particularly that first week in court. Her beautiful mum came with me on the days she couldn't be there because of her work commitments. It had been a very confronting and frightening time for me, not knowing what would come of it or how I was supposed to defend myself.

Things progressed very quickly, and it became quite evident that I would not be able to handle this one by myself. My dad decided that they had to come home to attend court with me, sit in the meetings with my accountant and solicitors, pick me up every time I fell, try to get me to eat, and for Mum to help look after my little girls while I attended court every day.

A Queens Council Barrister was representing the franchisor. This meant that I also had to get an equal-standing Queens Council Barrister to defend me. The cost for this was exorbitant. We are talking thousands of dollars per day, with additional costs every day they have to appear in court. Add to this my solicitors, who were putting together all of the information and doing all the research behind the scenes.

The court case went on for months. But I couldn't take the chance of not being represented properly. Aside from the initial claim and the injunction, they bombarded me with as many other charges as possible. As an example, they tried to have me charged with contempt of court because somebody took photos of my car parked close to the front of the office. They claimed that I was working. Kiama is a country town with only one main street where all the shops I would frequent for daily necessities were located. This was another fight I had to face because I wasn't working. In fact, I don't think I would have even been capable of working during this time. The court case literally took up every waking moment of my life as well as every ounce of energy I had. If anybody has been involved in a court case like this, you will understand the enormity of the emotional, physical, and mental exhaustion.

Every cent that I had made out of the business sale went towards fighting this case.

My mum was doing her best to look after my little girls when I couldn't. My dad was by my side through thick and thin. There wasn't a moment when he wasn't there for me. With stress and anxiety levels through the roof, I literally spent every waking moment swimming for my life against the tide, trying to work out how I was going to fix this. When it became apparent that this was going to drag on indefinitely, I took the advice of my solicitor and my accountant and put my company into voluntary administration, as the major claim was against my company, and I was the sole director.

I'd had zero choice in the matter by this stage anyway—I had nothing left. I had no money in the bank and was already hundreds of thousands in debt after selling my property.

Once the company was in the hands of an administrator, the court case was brought to a halt. However, because there were still claims against me personally and the purchasers of my business, the judge ordered us into mediation to bring it to a conclusion. We sat in that mediation room, my barristers, the franchisor and his barristers, the mediator, and my dad and I from 9 a.m. until midnight. It was one of the most draining and harrowing days of my life. It was ultimately determined that we all walk away. I paid the average of the six months' franchise fees owed, as I had been prepared to do from the beginning. Interestingly, a key point that was brought up as an explanation for what happened was that they wanted to make an example of me so that they didn't lose any more offices. *Pretty crazy, huh?* The mediator suggested there could be a reason why offices were choosing to leave.

The company didn't owe any money to creditors, so nobody missed out on being paid. I had also filled out personal bankruptcy forms, but luckily, I never sent them. At this point, I could so easily have left my company, let it go into liquidation, and filed for bankruptcy. If I had, I would not have all of the solicitors, barristers, accountancy fees, and administrators to pay off. I had already lost everything during this court case—my home, my savings, my company, my security, my confidence, my willpower, my independence, and my health for a while. So, I could probably have been excused for doing that. And I hadn't been able to earn an income during the almost 6 months of the court case. So why not? I had nothing left to lose. But I couldn't do it. My company, named after my daughters, was something that I fought so hard for. I wasn't going to let go of that.

I didn't believe anybody else should suffer financial loss from this situation either. I decided that I would pay back every cent of the debt I incurred fighting this case and buy my company back out of administration as soon as possible.

The end of the court proceedings would seem like it should have been a time of celebration, but it wasn't. I had hit rock bottom. A week after the court case finished, I was sitting in the park, playing with my daughters, and they asked me for ice cream. It was something so simple and small, yet I didn't even have the money to buy one. I had $1.76 in my bank account. I couldn't buy groceries, I ended up having to move into a property that my parents owned, and I relied upon them to help me with food for my daughters and I.

I had finally reached breaking point and had no idea how to recover from this. There were days and sometimes a week when I couldn't leave my house. Being found lying on the floor in the foetal position, crying to myself, was not one of my proudest moments. All I wanted to do was to be with my daughters and hide away from the world. I lost all drive to do or be anything. Yes, I was licking my wounds and likely feeling a little sorry for myself by this stage. But I also knew that I did not want this for my daughters. I wanted to be a good role model for them. I wanted to teach them to be strong and not give up. My daughters did not deserve to have a mum who would not do everything possible to give them the best life I could.

So, one morning, I got back up and decided that this would not be their life, nor would it be mine. The sooner I got back on my feet and back to work, the sooner I could repay my debt and start to rebuild my future. I made a decision that day and was fully aware that nobody was coming to rescue me. It was all up to me. I had no option but to start again and, in doing so, prove that I could do it for the sake of my daughters and everybody who had helped me and supported me through the nightmare. And, of course, I owed it to myself. I hadn't worked that hard to end up with nothing.

But I had soooo many questions running through my head. *Could I have done things differently? Could I have prevented this? Will it happen again?* And in the true essence of hindsight, yes, probably. I could have done many things differently, but I also knew that understanding that was a good start. And no, I would never let this happen again. Even asking those questions was useless because I had no way of changing things anyway. What's done is done. So, beating myself up was not the best use of my much-needed energy. And besides, I had already done plenty of that.

I went back to work as a contract agent with my old business, as we had negotiated that I would do right from the beginning. It was a bit of a rocky road for me, having to start again. Navigating my way through doubts and the emotional pressure I was putting on myself to get everything repaid as soon as possible. When you are looking at a mountain of debt every day and have no cash flow to do anything that you want to do, it gets quite overwhelming, especially after being in the position I had been in previously through hard work. This then affects your ability to function at your best and with your highest energy level. When you are working with people, it's hard to remain switched on, focused, and positive. But I was extremely determined, and therefore, I did everything I could to regain my previous level of performance.

As a contractor, there is no wage or retainer, so I still had no income unless I got results. Needless to say, time was of the essence! It was time to get started again.

It's impossible to know at the time things are happening to you, what's good and what's bad. Sometimes, the things that you strive the hardest for turn out to be the things that become your hardest lessons—your failures. And some of the worst things that happen turn out to be the best things to learn and evolve from.

For the next few months, I put everything into my career and my daughters while trying to find my mojo again. Until the tidal wave smashed down on me. Remember I said that I had hit rock bottom? Well, I hadn't. Until now.

CHAPTER 5

In the Blink of an Eye

On 16 July 2005, just a few months after the court case had finished, my heart broke into pieces. My hero, my dad, died suddenly. He was just 58 years old. This was when my world truly fell apart. I had been skiing for a week with my dad, my best friend Ali, our daughters, and one of my dad's mates, Mike. We had such an incredible time; the snow was thicker than it had been for many years, and life was starting to get back to some kind of normality.

Dad had bought an apartment in Jindabyne a few years prior, replacing his water skis with snow skis. It was covered in snow that week, so much so that the main electricity power station had shut down. This just added to the fun of the week for us, having to dig through the snow to get in and out. With no electricity to cook, we were barbecuing on the deck in the snow, and the kids were tobogganing down the street. Although, this also meant no hot water (this wasn't so fun!).

My dad and I were skiing black runs all day, every day, in fresh powder snow. And yet, there was no sign whatsoever of what was to come.

As I was just starting to see a little bit of light at the end of the tunnel, this little break was so needed for all of us. My mum was on holiday in Europe again, with her friends this time. It was school holidays, and Dad was taking some time away from the business to help look after my girls while I worked.

After an absolutely wonderful week away, we returned on Wednesday, had dinner with him on Thursday, and he and I took my daughters to see *Fantastic Four* at the movies. My dad then looked after my girls on Friday while I was at work, and their dad picked them up from him on Friday afternoon. At the time, Dad was trying to step away from his business and was looking to sell his site in Wollongong to a developer.

He absolutely adored his little granddaughters like nothing else. To say that they were spoiled rotten by my parents would be an understatement. They had a very special bond, and I am so deeply grateful that they got to meet and spend so much precious time with my dad and mum. Sadly, he never got to meet any of my nephews or his grandsons, but they know everything about him, as my brothers have made sure of that.

Dad and I often went to the gym together, and we were going to do that on Saturday morning and then have breakfast before I started my open homes for the day. I knew Dad was going to a friend's place to watch the football and have dinner and a drink on Friday evening, so I didn't speak to him after my girls had left. I lay in bed that night for hours, unable to sleep. It was the strangest feeling because I wasn't tossing and turning; I wasn't anxious about anything. I literally just could not sleep. The last time I remember looking at the clock, it was just after 3 a.m.

When my mobile rang, it was from a private number, so I didn't answer, but they proceeded to call again, and I knew something was wrong. A lady on the other end asked to speak to me. She asked me to come to the hospital straight away. I asked her what happened, and she said, "You just need to come to the hospital."

My initial thought was for my daughters, but if something had happened to them, my ex-husband would have called me straight away. It was then that I knew, without any hesitation, that it was my dad. But I couldn't even verbalise it, so I just asked, "Who?"

She said, "It's your dad. He's very sick. You need to come to the hospital."

I don't know how, but I knew that he had passed at that point. I was living on the same street as my parents. In fact, I was only seven doors away from their home. So, when I drove to the hospital, I drove past their house and noticed two ambulances parked outside. I didn't know what had happened; all the lights were on in the house, but nobody was home. I called my brothers and aunt to let them know, and I tried to call my mum, but with the time zones, she didn't get my calls until quite a bit later.

I arrived at the hospital, and as soon as I walked in, they ushered me through to another section. I was praying with every ounce of my being that I would walk through and see him sitting up on the bed with that smile in his eyes that I had seen the last time I had received a call such as this. But this time, that was not to be. There were police waiting inside the doors, and a nurse came up and told me that my dad had passed away. Although I knew, I just couldn't believe that he had died.

I was in complete shock. So, they took me inside to see him. He was laid out on a gurney, looking so peaceful that it looked like he was just asleep. I went over to him, and I just wrapped my arms around him and wouldn't let go. My brothers turned up not long after this, and my youngest brother collapsed when he heard the news. We were all so bereft and confused about how he had died. I was interviewed by the police, as is standard practice for all sudden deaths. I'm not quite sure why I took on this role, but possibly being the eldest. I asked them what had happened to my dad. I didn't understand the police involvement at that point, and I thought something terrible must have happened to him like a car accident on his way home or somebody had hurt him. But the nurses and paramedics assured me he had passed away under natural circumstances. He'd had a heart attack. Knowing this made me incredibly sad because living so close to my dad made it seem so wrong that I wasn't with him.

He was the most social person that I have ever known. He was rarely alone, always the life of the party, and always surrounded by people. And yet he had died alone. My daughters called him Party Pa because that's what he was to them—the life of the party. He saw them every day and always made sure that their time together was full of fun. He spent every moment he could with them. I had no idea how I was supposed to tell them they would never see him again. Having to do that was breaking my heart even more.

I needed to know details and timelines, who called the ambulance, etc. I think it helped me to understand what he went through. My dad had come home from dinner and gone to bed before waking up with chest pain a few hours later. He had called an ambulance himself, put his phone and his keys into his pocket, locked up the house, and stood waiting on the side of the street for them to turn up. My dad had been having a mild heart attack at home, but he had a major heart attack once they got him into the ambulance and started to prepare him for travel to the hospital. This had done so much damage to his heart by killing off 40 percent of the heart muscle that they could not bring his heart back into a regular rhythm, and they could not save him. He actually died in the ambulance right out the front of his home.

I felt so much guilt that I wasn't with him, that I should have been holding him and telling him how much I loved him. I just couldn't bear the thought of him dying alone. It has been something that I have struggled with for many years. It took us a couple of hours to get hold of our mum as she was in France having a lovely picnic with her friends. It was the most heartbreaking moment having to tell her over the phone that Dad had passed away. She was in total shock and denial, like the rest of us. She had to be sedated for the flight home.

We sat with our dad for hours that day, not wanting them to take him away. Just wanting an extra moment to hold his hand and talk to him. But obviously, it came to the point where we were told we had to leave. I don't remember much of the next couple of days as I was just so numb. I do remember coming home and curling up into a ball, feeling intense pain in my own chest. I felt like I couldn't breathe. Apparently, this happens to some people when you lose somebody that you are very close to. You experience the same physical pain. I didn't want my daughters to see or feel what I was feeling, as I already knew how much they would suffer when they found out. Telling my little girls that their beloved Party Pa had passed away was absolutely gut-wrenching.

Their dad and I told them, but they couldn't understand how he could have died when he wasn't sick. Or why the hospital couldn't make him better. They were just 5 and 8 and had shared so many special moments with their Nanma and Pa, who would take them on holidays and weekends away at every opportunity. I found my eldest around the side of the house later that day, writing a little note to her Pa in chalk on the side of the house. It said, *"I miss you, Party Pa,"* and it shattered me. Their little calling sign to each other was "Coooo-eee!" which is how they sent him off with their personal notes on his coffin.

We received lots of signs from him that week before the funeral. We found a little love heart on the floor, perfectly shaped out of tissue. We put it on some pink cardboard and laminated it—we still have it today. When we were choosing our songs for the funeral, it got too much for us, so I went and turned off the sound system. By the time I got back to the table, with about 12 people there, it turned back on again, and the song continued. I guess he wanted us to hear it until the end. There were many more, and I am still so fortunate to feel him around me all the time.

It took a couple of days for Mum to get home, and having to pick her up from the airport and drive her to the morgue to see him is still etched into my mind. It was so devastating for her to get that call when she was on the other side of the world.

Our dad was an incredibly generous and caring man, and his funeral was a massive testament to that. There were so many people who couldn't even fit inside but who chose to be there anyway. So many people came to show their love. My life and the lives of my family have never been the same, but for Mum, it was beyond bearable. Death has such a far-reaching ripple effect, and it seeps into every nook and cranny of life for those left behind.

I was doing everything I could to support my mum, who never fully recovered from the loss of our dad. Her health started to deteriorate from this point, both physically and mentally. And it goes without saying that it also hit me hard. I have never been as lonely as I was after losing Dad. For months, I would pick up my phone every day to call him. I cried myself to sleep most nights for years. I felt like I was swimming through mud, just trying to get through every day.

It is completely traumatising when someone dies suddenly, and adapting to life without them is so hard. The indescribable grief and pain are just the start. I am not sure where I would be today without my daughters, my brothers and sis-in-laws, my aunts, and my best friends Trina & Ali, who helped me through. My daughters were and still are everything I live for— loving and caring for them was my only remedy. I am truly fortunate to also have had Ali, who, to this day, is my rock. She helped me to keep moving forward through the murky waters until I could eventually see the shore again. She made sure I kept breathing, kept eating, and kept talking. She held me through many tears and was beside me every time I cried for help. Nothing has changed 18 years later, and she's still picking up the pieces, making me laugh, telling me when I'm out of line or when I need to stand up for myself. Everyone needs a friend like Ali.

To add to this year of absolute shittiness, my body also started to exhibit physical signs of the mental stress I was putting it through. I lost most of the hearing in my left ear (luckily, it's just the one side), so it's best to always sit to my right if you want me to hear your conversation and I now have constant tinnitus, which is the result of an autoimmune disease called Menière's Disease. It also causes balance issues and vertigo, which, fortunately for me, has not been constant but has certainly been triggered on many occasions over the years. Some of these occurrences have been severe vertigo attacks, rendering me unable to stand or even sit. I can't open my eyes or do anything but lie flat on my back in a dark room with my eyes closed to control the vomiting, nausea, and spinning room that comes along with it. If you've never had vertigo, it's like the days of being so drunk that the whole room is spinning, you can't walk straight, and when you go to sit on something, you miss it altogether and fall on the floor. And it doesn't stop when you sober up, and you don't get to enjoy the fun that usually precedes the spinning, nausea, and vomiting.

There is no cure for this, but I manage the symptoms through a combination of diet and removing as many sugars, toxins, and processed foods as I can from my diet, as they can feed autoimmune diseases. I also TRY to avoid caffeine, alcohol, and salt, which are meant to make it worse. But let's be real, I can't live without SOME caffeine in my life—coffee is my drug. And wine, I can't live without that either. I just have to limit myself nowadays and read the signs to cut back when I feel it starting to affect me.

Divorce. Financial ruin. Death. Disease

I still can't fathom how I survived that year, but I knew I had to do it for my dad, my mum and my daughters. Grief is truly one of the most difficult emotions to get through. I know everybody who has been through a loss like this will understand. Having to pick up the pieces and try to live a normal life again is impossible. Life cannot be normal again. You have to create a new life without that person in it. They say that strength is not doing what you can do; it's doing the things you think that you cannot do, and I believe that to be true.

I truly did not think I had it in me to return to work and continue on with life without my dad by my side. However, I knew that would be the last thing he would want for me and for my daughters. So, through many tears, frustrations, and days I could barely get out of bed, let alone sit in front of a client to discuss selling their home, I slowly worked my way back into making money again. It was probably one of the hardest things that I have ever done to get my mind back on track and to be able to focus on what I needed to do to fulfil my goal of being debt-free in the shortest possible space of time. I wanted so much to make my dad proud, and I knew that nobody could do that but me.

I had a choice after all of this had happened, and that choice was either to give up and just exist, or I could make a difference and fight back, swimming against the currents that seemed to be inexorably dragging me out to sea. I chose to swim.

After I came back to work, I found some kind of courage to do the things that I needed to do in order for me to get back on track. I put in the effort. I went back to basics, and I reached the ranking of number 12 in the state for Ray White Regional, New South Wales.

It took me almost five years to repay the debt, and I eventually bought my company back at a cost of over $100,000. It was worth every cent. I was back to a breakeven point—ground zero. A clean slate from which I could rebuild.

I was a single mum, juggling home duties and working long hours to somehow get us back on our feet. But it was sink or swim, and I knew that I just couldn't sink. Until we face a challenge that we think is insurmountable, we never really know how tough we are.

I spoke to my dad every day. Usually, a lot more than once a day, so breaking the habit of being able to pick up the phone and call him, asking his advice and running my decisions by him, telling him what my girls got up to and how things were going at work was one of the hardest habits I have ever had to break. When you have someone like that by your side, especially when it has been for the entirety of your life, it's that loss of communication and support, which is something I think most people also find so difficult to accept. Having to break the expectation of them always being there. You feel like you're floating, with no anchor, and second-guessing yourself in everything you do. I didn't think I'd ever have anyone who understood me like my dad did or would love me unconditionally as he always did. But I understand now that I was wrong. People will step up if you let them in. I'm one of those people who close off when I'm sad. So, it's been a lifelong journey for me to open up to others and allow them to help and support me when I need it most. I guess this book is my way of smacking myself in the face, unpacking my shit, and opening up in the biggest way possible. To the world…

See.

High achiever—I never do anything by halves.

Anyway… My dad still manages to find ways to guide me. The problem is, I don't always listen.

Side note: If I can advise any business owners on this, it's to organise a company power-of-attorney, giving somebody else access and ability to take over and run the business in your absence—if it's ever needed. Internet banking wasn't a thing then, so all of the accounts were frozen, and it took a long time for us to sort through the paperwork and the logistics around getting things transferred over to Mum's name and winding up the business. Keep all of your passwords and instructions somewhere for your family. Think about what it will look like from a business perspective for your family if you are no longer around.

My dad was his business. When he was alive, his business was worth approximately $2 million, but once he had passed, it was worth nothing. There weren't databases; he didn't use computers. Everything was either *scribbled in his little book or in his head. Without him to pass on all of his knowledge, clients, contracts, etc., it was basically nothing but goodwill.*

He was also extremely underinsured. He kept rescheduling meetings with his broker to fix this, but it never happened, which made it difficult for Mum to work out payment of mortgages on their properties, some of which they were in the process of buying and selling at the time of his passing. You don't want your family to go through this. If you don't have an up-to-date will, get one. Probate takes time, and until it's been granted, it doesn't give your family access to anything.

When we experience trauma and adversity, it's often very hard to see beyond the pain and discomfort that we're feeling at the time. But I have learned that the sooner we lean into it, rather than running away from it, and let ourselves feel all of the emotions and give ourselves the space to express the feelings they elicit, the quicker we can process it and begin the healing process.

It's so important that we process our emotions rather than burying them, as it's a crucial step towards healing. Recognising, understanding, and expressing our feelings is the best way to start moving through the pain and discomfort toward a better place and much-improved well-being.

The longer we bury our feelings and emotions and don't face our trauma or adversity, the more risk there is of developing psychological distress, physical illness, relationship issues, unhealthy coping mechanisms, and a negative effect on mental health.

It took me a long time to realise that this was my pattern, I have a tendency to bury everything until I get to the stage where I feel like I'm going to burst. And usually, I do, literally. I randomly burst into tears and cry for days… But I always feel so much lighter and have more clarity afterward.

Everyone needs a good cry now and then! It's so cleansing.

CHAPTER 6

Learning From the Past

Your power does not come from not failing. Your power exists because failure hasn't stopped you.

When the Court case was settled, I told my dad and my accountant two things I would never do again: own a business and join a Franchise. They said, "Never say never." And they were right. Turns out I lied. Inadvertently, of course.

After almost five years, I made a decision that I did not think I would ever make again. I chose to go back into business AND join another franchise. As a contractor, I was technically running a business within a business. But it was time to start again and grow my own team under a new brand. Glutton for punishment? Maybe, but I had started to rebuild my life and paid off my debt, and that desire to be a leader and to grow something from scratch was back with a vengeance.

As broken as I had been, I knew that I still had so much more to give. My daughters were growing up, and I had also met somebody amazing who I was in a serious relationship with. With their support, I opened a new agency and started to build this business from a complete start-up. To say that I was nervous would be an understatement. I had a lot of mental obstacles to overcome, but I never doubted my ability to build a successful business again. And this time, I would do it better, with all intentions of making it bulletproof.

When I opened this agency, I started with just one employee. I chose not to buy a rent roll but rather to grow one organically this time around. I don't think that I have ever worked harder than I did to get this business off the ground. I was working 15-hour days, seven days a week to ensure that we became financially stable as quickly as possible.

Still being a very hands-on mum, doing my best to ensure that my daughters also had time, I worked in the office until they were home from school or after-school activities. I spent time with them, and then I worked until the early morning hours to keep on top of everything. The 1:00 and 2:00 a.m. emails to the team were legendary, and they would often ask whether I ever slept (this from someone who has always loved her sleep!). A girl's gotta do what a girl's gotta do though, right?

My partner, who would become my second husband, did interstate fly-in-fly-out work. So we never actually lived together permanently in our ten years as a couple. This meant that I was still doing pretty much everything that needed to be done at home: picking up dog poop, putting bins out, cooking, cleaning, shopping, washing, kid taxi, homework duties, walking the dog, washing the car (blah blah blah). I mean, women CAN multitask, right?

Except it wasn't as easy as that seemed. So many people would constantly say to me, "I don't know how you do it, Marn." And the truth is, I was mostly hanging onto everything by the skin of my teeth. The kids were always late to school, and homework and assignments often weren't done until the night before, if at all. I'd be running between appointments to drop them off at their after-school activities and on the phone with clients the whole time. Holidays and eating out were always interrupted by work calls and urgent emails. We got takeaway far too often, and the laundry would spill out into the hallway before I got to it. I literally did not stop. From 7.30 am to 1.00 am (on a good day!) I would be like a mouse on one of those little round treadmills. But it was the only reality I knew at that time, and it was what I had to do to make sure that all aspects of my life, business, and family were being taken care of.

I had the working mum guilt to battle with, but for years, it was my normal routine, and I'm just so thankful that my daughters were able to adjust and appreciate what I was doing and why I was doing it. They spent lots of time with me at the office and helped me with work. We had quality time together at every opportunity, and they both have an incredible work ethic and successful careers behind them now. My youngest is already a business owner at 23, and my eldest is living her dream in a career that she has wanted since she was a child. I guess it's a similar pattern as my years spent with my dad in his business.

Starting a business all over again made me miss my dad even more. He had been my mentor and my safety net throughout my life, and he was definitely my source of downloads and questions when it came to business. So, it was a much more daunting process, and there were many times of overwhelm, second guessing myself, and delays in taking the action I should have been taking at the beginning.

Starting the business from scratch meant that there was no income for a period of time, in addition to the cost of fit-out, upfront rent, and wages. This is in comparison to previously buying an existing business that was already generating income. So, I started in the red (my trigger colour, remember!), which meant that I had to get out of that as soon as possible—quick income and low overheads. Essentially, the only solution for this was me generating as much income as possible as soon as I could.

I was determined to grow the business in a measured and controlled way. I had big goals, of course, but I also knew that I needed to take my time and ensure I had the capital to take it where I wanted it to go.

I did a leadership and management course before opening the business this time. This gave me an incredible grounding and helped me to set the right foundations and build a growth plan for my business moving forward. It also gave me a network of other new business owners to keep in touch with, brainstorm ideas, and ask questions if needed. Still, the first couple of years were like a rollercoaster ride—sometimes thrilling, sometimes scary, sometimes inverted, sometimes holding on like grim death!

To be fair, I was finding my feet again and probably spreading myself too thin if I am being honest. But if you've ever been in a position where you have no money and can't pay your bills, you'll understand the level of fear around that ever happening again. You quickly discover how hard you can push yourself and what you're capable of.

I've never been money-driven. However, after losing everything, I definitely developed some nervousness around money. It created a new perspective on having a financial safety net. Growing a business from scratch is a constant juggle between generating income, covering costs, and investing in recruitment. But, no matter how hard you work, there are only so many hours in a day, and relying on just one person to generate the income is obviously limiting. So recruitment was a priority fairly quickly.

Because I was in a regional area, there were a lot of difficulties in finding salespeople and property managers. It took time to find the right people, which meant that my recruitment plan was a bit hit-and-miss to start with. But, consistency and persistence are the keys to a strong recruitment plan for any business. It's a matter of always being prepared if someone comes along out of the blue, nurturing and maintaining contact with prospective recruits you've identified as a potential, and constantly thinking ahead, as it's not a good idea to wait until you're desperate to fill a position before you start looking. Every person that you meet is an opportunity to consider. Most of the best people in my business came from out of the industry. With the right people, training is the easy part.

I believe in a very open and transparent workplace, and it is important for me when I bring new people into the business that they fit in and get on with the rest of the team. I also believe that the goal of any business is to become an attraction business. Not just for clients and customers, but also for staff. When this happens, you will find that people will come to you without you having to actively seek out people for expansion. It is becoming more and more common for people looking for a new opportunity to research and choose who they want to work with rather than the other way around.

So always make sure your business is showing up and that the community and your staff are talking about you in a very positive and encouraging way. Social media plays an important role in this as well. Potential recruits will be watching your socials to learn more about you and your business. Showing that you promote fun, wellness, and community involvement, or whatever sets you apart and keeps your team happy, will give them an idea of what it's like to work for you. This is essentially how my team grew.

While it might not suit everybody, a social workplace worked for me. We did a lot of team bonding and team-building exercises to further develop our trust and confidence in each other. This created such a strong impression within the community, and people saw my business as being a great place to work. The perception amongst potential new team members was also that we were a standout business in the area. This environment and its culture resulted in the existing staff being my best recruiters.

Growing a rent roll organically was my next challenge, as it was something new for me and something that I had to consider in the recruitment process as well. Operating in a small town meant that there were limited investment properties. There were also a lot of real estate agencies, so it was a competitive environment we were trying to tap into. Having the right team was a big part of the success of this department as it's imperative that they are able to bring in new business as well as service and maintain existing clients. Until the rent roll reaches a certain number of managements, it's hard to justify splitting those roles. Over time, we grew to create a really strong team who built a solid reputation for professionalism and personalised client service, and a healthy and dollar-productive property management portfolio.

I went on to trade for three years under this initial franchise, building a team of seven plus myself. We had developed good market share and gained more traction every year. But I knew that I needed a change to help boost my business profile and give me a further point of difference. I had always admired the McGrath brand, and John McGrath was one of my role models in real estate business and training. Due to my previous experience, there was a lot of uncertainty about whether I should take the chance and rebrand or continue as I was and play it safe. Playing it safe is not something I tend to do often, though. So, I decided to change but waited until my current franchise agreement had expired. I also advised them face to face and in writing, very clearly, that I would finalise the franchise before making any changes.

My next obstacle was getting McGrath to consider my office. That wasn't as easy as I thought it was going to be! There weren't many McGrath offices in regional areas at the time, so a lot of their criteria weren't quite met on my part. But I was so determined that I just kept pushing.

After many meetings with the corporate team, I received a call from John McGrath's PA one afternoon, asking me whether I would be available to have breakfast with John the next morning in Sydney. *Ohhhhhh! This must be the final test. Make or break time.* Was I confident? Hell no! I was sh*#ting bricks! But I knew that I could do it… somehow. I had to. There was no Plan B this time around, either.

After a dozen or so outfit changes, organising somebody to get my girls to school, and a 4 a.m. wake-up, I arrived in plenty of time for our 7 a.m. breakfast meeting. Having a breakfast meeting is not always ideal when trying to remain professional and impress somebody. Eating and talking at the same time—this may not end as well as I had hoped. I spent my entire waiting time perusing the menu over and over, trying to work out what I could eat with as much decorum as the meeting deserved. But I was wasting energy worrying. Because I have to say that from the moment he arrived, John was so humble and friendly, and within five minutes, he had me totally relaxed. While we were going through many business discussions and talking about my plans for expansion into other areas, he asked me a very funny question about the South Coast. It was about a little rumour that I had also heard before about Berry. But it made me laugh coming from him. Anyway, for some reason, I knew at that point that I had made the right decision, wanting to own a McGrath agency. Being real is the best personality trait for me.

Oh, and before you ask—what happens in Berry, stays in Berry!

Anyway, I must have made a decent impression, as eventually, I was accepted into the network. *Yesssss!* A little lesson here, too. Don't just take no for an answer. When you want something enough, never stop trying to turn a no into a yes. Do what it takes, with respect, to prove how much you're prepared to put into changing the outcome through extra effort, thinking outside the box, and persistence.

My Kiama office became the 50th office within the McGrath group in 2012. Within that first year trading under their brand, my team and I managed to triple our income. The brand also attracted a number of high-performing contract agents who wanted to be a part of our team. My team was very excited about the new brand as well, which was important to me.

As we expanded, culture became even more important than it was before. To run a large team and maintain a happy work environment, the way everyone interacts and sees themselves as fitting in becomes a fundamental priority. Communication, collaboration, and teamwork were essential, and allowing them all to have a voice meant that nobody had any reason to feel unheard or unseen. Although we all focus mainly on recruitment, I believe that retention is just as important, if not more important.

The business really took off from this point, and I was in full performance mode, running at my peak both as a selling principal and as a business owner. I had promoted one of my most valued and trusted team members to Operations Manager, and with her by my side to manage and support both myself and the team moving forward, we were able to expand to our next phase sooner rather than later.

In 2014, I opened my second office in Berry on the New South Wales South Coast. This was the 60th McGrath office at the time. When we talk about manifesting and creating opportunities, this was another perfect example for me of how the universe will provide if we're ready. An office in Berry was always in my business plan, but I hadn't determined exactly when and how. One day, an ex-colleague and sales coach I had previously worked with came to see me. He had been operating an extremely successful independent boutique real estate agency in the Berru region, and he wanted to sell the business. This was purely a sales agency with 15 properties listed for sale at the time. I knew that if I could take over these listings and sell them under my brand, that would give me an incredible foothold in the local market, with great exposure and proven results, before we opened the office. So, I took the opportunity and did just that. I managed to sell 12 of the 15 listings over the first six-month period, and McGrath Berry suddenly had a strong presence within the local property market. We were then able to leverage off these listings to attract and sign further sellers so that we could open the office with a track record and new listings ready to go.

While this was a challenging task to keep on top of my core area in Kiama and still service these listings, which were located quite a distance apart, it served me well in building our profile quickly in the new area.

The Berry office was in a rural location, so it encompassed a lot of large properties, often in remote locations. This was a completely different market from Kiama, which was mostly made up of residential coastal properties. In order to make having a second office as cost-effective as possible, we ran most of the administrative support and property management from the head office in Kiama. The Berry office was a fully functioning sales office with a receptionist who did the day-to-day administration for the sales team. Having two offices in very different locations took up a good deal of my time, but it was worth it for the amazing experience I had selling so many stunning properties in these locations.

My team had grown to 20, and I was fortunate (or opportunistic once again!) to find a fantastic Licensee-In-Charge for the Berry office around the same time I was looking for sites for the office. Having trusted staff in managerial positions was imperative as it allowed me to continue to focus on generating income, nurturing and mentoring the team, and building the business.

That nine-year period in this business brought many career highlights for me. We hit many goals and achieved so much more than I could have ever hoped for. We were recognised for a number of awards, and we were incredibly successful with them. The first year that we were nominated in The Illawarra and South Coast Local Business Awards as Most Outstanding Real Estate Agency, we won. The next year, we were nominated in the same category for the second largest award—Overall Business of the Year—and we won both. This was an awesome achievement, and I was ridiculously proud of my team, who all contributed to the award. Standing on that stage with them made everything so worth all of the effort.

We skipped a year then—no awards! I'll tell you about that year in the next chapter. But the next year, we were nominated again—this time, it was me as well as the office. Me, for Businessperson of the Year—the biggest award, the Gold Logie of the ceremony, so to speak. I was truly grateful and blown away just to have had my name read out in the top 5. But when they called out my name as the winner, and there I was—large as life on the big screen—I was speechless. No, I mean really speechless. I hadn't even written a speech as I honestly didn't think I had any chance of winning. *Oh shittttt!* I had to get up in front of thousands of people and hope that something intelligible came out of my mouth. But it had been such a hard year personally that I had no words. I had just lost my mum. I had survived a stalker. My second marriage had just broken down. Yes, I know I just threw a few bombshells in there—we will get to those in the next chapters—but you can see why I was an emotional mess on stage. To be honest, I can't even remember what I spoke about.

But the fact remained: I had won. I was absolutely so very proud and grateful. Having had a lifetime goal of being a business owner, this was something that I could never have imagined in my wildest dreams. To this day, I have so much appreciation, love, and respect for every person who ever worked in my business, and I know that every one of them had some impact on this result.

Who'd have ever imagined that my childhood dream of business ownership would end up being celebrated, validated, and recognised in a way such as that? Woooo-bloody-hoooo!

My business and I had come a very long way, and I was super proud of what we had all achieved. I think it's important to give back to your team when they come in every day and give their all to you. The more appreciation you show, the more effort they will want to give because they want to make you proud. And needless to say, after this series of awards, we certainly celebrated together.

"Empowering those around you to be heard and valued makes the difference between a leader who simply instructs and one who inspires."
– Adena Friedman, CEO

I could never have achieved what I did without my team supporting me all the way.

I also remarried during these years, and we rebuilt two homes, renovated another, and enjoyed a lot of fun and adventure, trying hard to keep all the balls in the air as we juggled our way through our 10 years together.

CHAPTER 7

Coping With Shadows

It was an interesting juxtaposition during those years as a successful businesswoman next to the craziness and often traumatic events still happening in my personal life. Looking from the outside in, nobody except family and close friends really knew what was going on for me during that time. I was determined not to let my business be adversely affected, so I kept things within my little sphere of influence as much as possible.

As I mentioned in the last chapter, I lost my beautiful mum who tragically passed away, I had a stalker, I ran a marathon with a torn Achilles tendon and a botched training regime, and I had spinal surgery, then rode in a 215 km charity cycling event four weeks later, I also had a hysterectomy and major prolapse reconstruction surgery, I took in a foster child and my second marriage broke down.

Deep breaths... *One. Two. Three.*

Oh, and this is just the stuff I'm willing to share. I only told you about the good stuff in the last chapter. After all, it can't be all doom and gloom! But wow, what a ride my personal life was during those successful years in business.

I'll start with the stalker. I'm sure that's what you are most curious about. It was a bad stalker, one who went to prison.

As a real estate agent, we are always in the public eye. Our phone numbers and email addresses are plastered everywhere, our work address is easy to find, and we always put photos of ourselves in papers, on signboards, brochures, and online. People know where we will be on a Saturday and sometimes mid-week too, as we advertise our open homes with the addresses everywhere. I'd had a few other issues in the past, but I knew from the start that this one was different. It started after a full-page profile photo of me featured in the local newspaper, an introductory promotion showcasing our rebrand to McGrath.

I was in the office working late when I received a phone call from a man telling me that he thought I was attractive. He said that he had seen my photo in the paper. He also told me that he had seen my "smile" that day. I wasn't sure whether he meant in person or in the photo. He asked me if I was single, and I told him I wasn't single, thanked him for his kind words, and told him that I had to go. He kept pushing to talk, but I ended up politely excusing myself and hanging up.

I often worked very late at night by myself in the office, which was situated on a prominent roundabout on the main street of our town. The whole shopfront was floor-to-ceiling glass all the way around, so it was a little bit like a fishbowl—we had no window cards or anything in the windows blocking visibility. With an open-plan office and all the lights on, everyone could see in, and it would be obvious to anyone outside when you were preparing to leave.

When I walked out of the office that night, I had a really strange feeling. I felt like I was being watched. I would always park behind our office in a laneway, which was very dark at night, so getting to the car and getting in quickly was a priority that evening. The call had come from a private number, so I couldn't check it out, and after a few days, I forgot all about it.

Then a week later, I was at a barbecue with some friends on a Saturday night. My mobile rang at about 9 o'clock with a private number, and I instinctively answered it, unsure whether it could be one of my daughters or my mum. When I picked up the phone, a man was moaning and repeatedly saying my name. I could hear him masturbating.

I quickly tried to pass the phone to my husband or a friend, but he hung up after he realised that I was no longer on the line. Everybody was making a joke, and I can't blame them because I would probably have done the same if I wasn't the one on the receiving end. At that point, I hadn't put two and two together and just thought that it was some random being a grub. But hearing him say my name in the context of what he was doing left me feeling really uncomfortable, and it made my skin crawl.

That Monday morning, I was running into the office for our sales meeting, and my mobile rang again, so I answered without even looking at the screen. I assumed it would be a work-related call. It was the same guy doing the same thing, but this time, he was telling me all the things he would do to me.

The nature of this call was much more threatening, as the way he spoke was with absolute intent that these things would happen. He was giving very vulgar descriptions of what he was planning to do to me. What he was saying were not normal sexual behaviours—they were animalistic and extremely violent sexual acts. Again, he hung up when he heard other people around.

I decided that it was time to call the police to report him. As part of my statement, I had to tell them exactly what he said and did on the phone. At first, I think they thought it was just somebody playing a prank, but as soon as I started telling them about what was said in the last phone call, I could see them both looking a bit shocked. They said they would investigate and track the number and call me once they found out who it was.

In the meantime, they told me not to be in places by myself and not to place any more photos in the paper or elsewhere. But I'm a real estate agent. That's what we do!

During this time, my real fear was for the safety of my teenage daughters because we mostly lived alone while my husband was interstate working. I spent long hours at the office, and they often came home from school and were in the house by themselves in the afternoons. I had no idea whether I had been followed home at some stage because if somebody knows where you work, it's not hard for them to follow you home. I wasn't prepared to take any chances with them, so I made other arrangements for my daughters when I wasn't home.

I also stopped answering private numbers. To this day, I still will not answer a private number. If it's a legitimate caller, they can leave a message, and I will call them back.

Over the next few weeks, I received random calls asking strange questions about particular properties and open homes through the office, so it was hard to tell whether they were legitimate or not. My senses were on high alert at this point, and I knew never to say yes when somebody asked me whether a property was vacant, for example. I also had to take somebody with me if I was inspecting a property with somebody I had not previously met.

Aside from my daughter's and my safety, I was conscious that I had a mainly female team of beautiful women. Their security was also a big concern, so we put measures in place in the business to protect everybody. This kind of thing highlights the dangers of our industry—we go to vacant homes and meet people we have never met before. We go knocking on strangers' doors, and we go to meet strangers on the assumption that we are appraising their homes. It is a high-risk career when you consider how often we are likely to be in risky situations, especially with some of the very remote properties we were selling in the country areas. Many of those properties had no phone service and were accessed via dirt roads not used by the public. So, ensuring my team's safety became paramount.

We implemented a register at the front desk where everyone had to put in their movements, the contact information of the person they were meeting, the anticipated time of return, and where they were going. We also had a safe phrase that everybody in the office knew, plus we had a new protocol for conducting open homes and doing remote inspections in pairs. I advised my team to stand out on the driveway when meeting new people, not waiting inside the home. If it was a vacant property, or even if it was a property where nobody was around and a man turned up on his own, or they didn't feel comfortable with the buyers for any reason, they could tell the clients to go inside and start looking around so they could then call or text the office.

Our safe phrase was to call or text and ask for a folder. If they were uncomfortable and wanted somebody else from the office to be with them, they would ask for the purple folder. We would immediately send somebody straight to the property to join them. If they were in a situation where they knew they were in danger and needed the police, then they would ask for the red folder, and we would initiate that. With the remote properties, we would make sure our male agent was available to go with the females wherever possible.

Ultimately, it's our job as leaders to do all we can to keep our team safe while they are undertaking their duties as an employee.

The police had started an investigation to track down the caller, but it took a while. before I got the information back. It was pretty scary knowing that somebody out there was possibly stalking me. When I received a call from the police officer investigating the calls after they traced the number, he advised that there were other investigations involving the same person coinciding with mine. The creep had also been calling two other women, another real estate agent and another business owner.

At the time, he had a record, having previously been convicted of crimes relating to drugs and armed robbery but nothing sexual. While they were building a case against him for the threatening phone calls, stalking, and other charges, we were again advised to take great care in our movements and to be very mindful of being alone with people we didn't know.

One evening, while the girls and I were home alone, our dog started barking wildly from inside, and one of my daughters woke up, yelling to me that she could hear somebody running across the deck. I had nothing but a baseball bat, so I ran downstairs with my bat and got the girls together to make sure that they were safe, and we proceeded to look around the house and let the dog outside. He was running around, still barking, but nobody was in the yard then. I turned on the alarm downstairs, and the girls came and slept with me upstairs, but needless to say, we didn't get much sleep. I couldn't be sure that it hadn't been a possum or something, so I didn't report it at the time because I had no evidence that anybody had actually been there. Or so I thought.

Two days later, my eldest daughter was in the shower and started yelling at me. I went in, and she said, "Mum, look at the window." Because of the steam in the room, it had highlighted handprints on the window. We also noticed then that the screen had been removed. I went outside and walked down the side, and there were large boot prints in the mud leading up to the window. The screen was sitting on the ground under the window. We called the police, and they came and took fingerprints, but it was raining, and there had been two days in between hearing the noises and footsteps running across the deck, so I don't believe they were able to get a clear fingerprint. This obviously scared the hell out of us.

When somebody tries or succeeds in breaking into your home, it takes away your sense of safety and security. It leaves you feeling vulnerable and frightened. None of us were comfortable staying there for a while, especially on our own. But it was our home, so we really had no choice in the matter. We did spend a few nights staying with my mum, though. Luckily, I had a king-sized bed because there ended up being the three of us plus a dog in there every night for quite a while.

The next call that I got from the police was to advise me that before they could build their case and arrest him, this man sexually assaulted one of the women by knifepoint. Although horrendous, thankfully, she managed to escape, and he was arrested and charged. We were preparing to go to court to testify about our experiences with him. However, at the last minute, he changed his plea to guilty on the sexual assault charges. This meant that our evidence was not heard in court. I don't know the full series of events in this regard, so I have to be very careful about how much information I give. But it is my understanding that they also found rope and tape, and other items believed to show evidence of intent to kidnap at his home. He was given 8 to 10 years in prison.

While he was in prison, I moved about three or four times. This turned out to be a blessing for me. He was released early, but I wasn't advised that he had been released. I'm not too sure about the other victims. He then went on to commit some extremely vicious and serious sexual crimes. I'm not going to mention what they were or his name, but they were abhorrently disgusting in nature, and I am still heartbroken for the victims of this monster.

I had never really understood the concept of survivor's guilt until this happened. It's such a strange feeling to be so grateful and overcome with relief that it wasn't me or my family, but I felt guilt that it wasn't me, that other people had been attacked, resulting in their lives being changed forever. I guess this is one of those situations I mentioned whereby I was a victim.

He was caught again and sent back to prison, where he has since passed away—which is the only thing that helps me sleep at night. Being in a situation like that is hard to explain. You're always having to look over your shoulder, never knowing whether somebody is going to be there. It's a terrifying experience that can cause ongoing fear and vulnerability. In a way, it affects your right to freedom, to be and do what you want without having to consider who may be watching or whether you're in danger.

I was very fortunate to have a supportive family and understanding team around me who took up the slack when needed and allowed my daughters to become my priority whilst this was happening.

CHAPTER 8

A Heartbreaking Farewell

4 October 2016

The day my beautiful mum passed away.

The next tidal wave.

As I have previously mentioned, Mum missed our dad a lot. It wasn't very long after Dad passed that Mum told us that she had been diagnosed with an autoimmune disease called Giant Cell Arteritis, which is an inflammation of the lining of your arteries. Most often, it affects the arteries in your head, especially those in your temples close to the optic nerve. It's quite a rare disease and one where there were not a lot of treatment options. But, the autoimmune disease could have resulted in blindness and further brain issues if untreated. So, she was going to a specialist who prescribed a new drug called methotrexate. I believe it was still in the trial phase when Mum started on it. This drug was supposedly successful in treating many people effectively.

Unfortunately, Mum was one of the rare ones who suffered side effects. She started to have significant problems with her lungs and her breathing, and by the time we were referred to another specialist, who told her that it may have been due to the methotrexate, her lungs had been severely damaged.

She was then diagnosed with Pulmonary Fibrosis, which they said was untreatable. The only option for her at that point would have been a lung transplant. However, she had just turned 66, and the cut-off age for a lung transplant is 65. Plus, she was pretty sick by this point, and an operation as big as that may not have been possible.

Toward the end with Mum, she was finally referred to a renowned specialist in this field, who was situated at RPA (The Royal Prince Alfred Hospital). When we went to see him, he took a scan of her lungs, and he was quite perplexed at the previous notion that the methotrexate caused it. He told us that if he had seen her sooner, he could have taken a biopsy of her lungs to determine exactly what was causing the Fibrosis. Unfortunately, by this time, Mum was far too sick to undergo anything like that.

Having been to many different specialists and through miles of testing with her, I was quite sure that there had been a number of misdiagnoses and a lack of proper investigation and treatment throughout my mum's health journey. But as angry and resentful as I was at the time, I had to let go of it as there was nothing I could do to change the outcome. I wish that I had picked up on what was happening sooner and been able to do something more about it. But my mum was pretty stubborn, too. By the time we got her to get a second opinion, it was too late. Her lungs continued to worsen. With Pulmonary Fibrosis, the lungs become scarred and turn spongy; therefore, they cannot function effectively. The average survival time after a diagnosis of Pulmonary Fibrosis is between three to five years.

Initially, Mum could manage to get through the day and just have oxygen now and then when she needed a top up. But as time went on, she contracted colds and lung infections, which did more damage and formed more scar tissue in her lungs. Eventually, she had to be on oxygen full-time—when she was asleep and when she was awake. This was tragic for a very proud, active, and independent woman. It got to the point where my mum could not look after herself. Her lungs were so bad that the oxygen wasn't helping, and her effort to take herself to the toilet or walk across the room was just too much. We got in-home care for her to help with things like cleaning and shopping, and we all tried to be there as often as we could to assist with everything else.

She went to the doctors one day for a checkup, and they checked her oxygen levels and called an ambulance to take her straight to palliative care. It was devastating for us. Although we knew she was very sick, we certainly didn't expect things to go downhill so quickly.

But the thing was, Mum was such a strong person that as soon as they put her on pure oxygen, she started to improve. After about four or five weeks in palliative care, they told us she couldn't stay there any longer. They weren't equipped to look after people for more than a week or so, which is a very sad thing to consider. Mum needed full-time care, and trying to get that for her at home was proving extremely difficult. She eventually needed to go into a facility, which was absolutely horrible considering that she was still in her 60s and had been quite fit and healthy not that long ago.

The facility was a Medical & Aged Care facility. So, Mum had a good 20 years on the majority of people there. This was really hard on her mentally, and the nursing staff, while they were mostly good with her, didn't have sufficient time to look after someone with her medical issues. She needed somebody available to attend to her regularly, as she couldn't even get out of bed on her own. Having to live like this, needing people to help you with everything, with no privacy, and having no quality of life resulted in our mum deciding that she had had enough.

As a family, we couldn't bear the thought of losing Mum this young, but we also could not bear to see her go through what she went through, day in and day out, just to stay alive and lay in a bed all day, every day. Mum had decided it was time for her to go and be with Dad, but for us, allowing her to go and telling her that it was okay for her to go was the hardest thing my brothers and I have ever had to do.

I slept beside my mum the nights before she passed. She woke briefly on the final morning and held my hand. As she started to go, I was alone with her as my brothers had not yet arrived. I was terrified. They were both on their way, but my aunt had just arrived, so she sat on my mum's other side as she struggled, and we both held her hands and told her it was okay to let go.

One of the biggest things I had trouble dealing with, losing Dad, was not being with him when he took his last breath. For years, I felt guilty that I wasn't with him so I could hold his hand and let him know that I was by his side. But after going through this with Mum and watching her go, hearing her fighting to take those last breaths absolutely tore me apart. I hated seeing her the way she was, but it still wasn't easy letting her go and seeing her final moments. I guess it also made me realise that there was a reason Dad didn't call me that night. I'm sure he didn't want me to see him going through this.

I kept praying for Dad to come and take her, and in those final moments, sunlight suddenly filled the room, and a little bird landed on the windowsill. I know in my heart that Dad was coming to get her, and I feel some peace knowing they are now together again.

I miss them so much, but I am truly so grateful for the time that I had them.

Grief is like the ocean.
It comes in waves.
Sometimes, when you least expect it.
Other times, it never leaves.
It can be calm, like a beautiful memory.
Or it can be overwhelming,
Leaving you numb.
It's a bittersweet reminder
Of what you had.
Memories to treasure.

There's no magic wand
To take the pain away.
All we can do is to swim
And face another day.

CHAPTER 9

The Healing Power of Movement

I discovered many years ago that the best antidepressant for me is exercise, so it was essential that it became part of my daily routine. But sometimes (often), I take it a little too far. By pushing myself to extremes, I feel nothing but physical pain at that time—it takes my mind off everything else. That's better than using drugs or alcohol, right? Or food?

I played a lot of competitive sports, love water and snow skiing, lifted pretty heavy weights, and kept reasonably fit, but I'm not a runner. As in, I hate it. But for some very odd reason, I decided that a marathon would be on my bucket list. Pretty dumb, really. I thought bucket lists were meant to be all fun stuff! I think I wanted to do it because I knew it would push me mentally and physically, and I never thought I would ever be able to do one. I know that doesn't make sense to a lot of people, but being the way I am, it makes perfect sense to always be challenging myself, proving I can break through my own limitations, and showing myself that I can do anything I set my mind to.

Take heights as another example. I'm terrified of heights. I literally freeze when I am in a tall building or standing on a mountain. So, I did a bungee jump, went skydiving (tandem, of course!), and climbed a very big mountain or two—in fact, lots of these, in an attempt to overcome my fear. It didn't really work. It didn't take away the fear. I still hate heights. But at least I know that it's no longer a limiting belief for me. I can no longer tell myself that I can't do those things! Because I have.

So anyway, same concept.

I happened to mention my goal of running a marathon to my gym bestie at the time, who generously offered to do it with me. *Oh dayummm!* So now it wasn't just on my list; I had put it out there, and now I had to do it. Together, we started a training program and booked ourselves in for the Gold Coast marathon, which was coming up in a few months. Neither of us liked running; it was more a nice time to chat and get coffee afterward. We trained as much as we were able, but to be honest, our program was definitely not what everybody recommends you do before running a marathon. Particularly for me, as I ended up with a tear in my Achilles tendon on my left foot and a cruciate ligament injury on my right. This rendered me pretty much lame, if I'm being honest. Every run was painfully hard. We started out doing 5 km loops. Sometimes, we would even walk these. On weekends, we aimed for a bit longer run. We just didn't always get there. We did one 15 km run, then we managed to complete a half marathon as part of our training schedule. Surprisingly, we completed it in a half-decent time. It must have been the pasta and the duck fat potatoes we had the night before the race.

Then, we did the longest run—25 km. I struggled with this big time! I walked a fair bit, I'll admit. I think I needed more duck fat potatoes beforehand; that's probably why. But, seriously, my feet hurt. Each time I ran, they became more inflamed. So, trying to walk each morning before the tendons warmed up was agony. It sounds like warming up a car before you hit the racetrack, doesn't it? It kinda was.

I went to the physio to get some dry needling and other treatments. He told me that I had two options.

1. Pull out of the marathon.
2. Stop training, let them heal for six weeks, then go and run the marathon.

Hmmmm.

If anyone has ever run a marathon before, you will know that you are meant to do between 32 and 35 km in training, and then you taper back down in the two weeks leading up to the race. You don't run the marathon before you run the marathon (I had so many people tell me that!). But you do get closer than 25 km, especially six weeks out, and with instructions to do very minimal, if any, running in between. But after deciding to do it, there was no way that I was pulling out. Regardless of our haphazard efforts at training, we talked ourselves up and didn't let ourselves believe that we couldn't do it. Not for a second.

You can probably tell by now that my running buddy also fell in line with my new training schedule. We continued with 5 km loops and managed to run around 12 km once on a Sunday in those six weeks. Our little mantra was we just need to keep the legs ticking over. We both believed that we were capable of doing that.

When you embark on a big physical challenge such as this, it is honestly so much of what is in your head that will decide the outcome. Your mind will give up before your body. If you can remain strong in your mind and determined to succeed, then you are capable of doing anything. A bit like running a business, I guess.

Our brain is wired to prevent us from getting hurt. So, as soon as we experience pain (mental and physical), it sends messages to the body to try to stop you from continuing as It's trying to keep you safe. So, you just need to override that program somehow.

The day finally came, and we arrived at the marathon. We had pasta, white bread sandwiches with honey, bananas, and anything carb-loaded the day before. *Not sure why; people just told us that we needed to carb-load!*

My gym buddy was a better runner than me, so it wasn't long before she pulled ahead. I was happy as I just needed to plod along and was facing a big mental barrier by that stage, too. My mind started to recognise that I had never run that far before. And the little b*#ch in my head kept reminding me of that. "She" was saying, *You're tired, you're in pain, you've tried,* and *It's okay to pull out now.* But I know what I'm like, and the other voice in my head that pushes me to never give up would have berated me for years to come, which was much worse. I would have just had to do it all again to shut it up. So, I kept going.

There's no need to give you a full narrative of my whole race, but the one thing I found truly astounding was how your body can find more fuel in the tank when you think it is completely depleted. It revisited my emotionally depleted state after the year of hell. I found more in the tank then, and I found more in the tank again. When I turned that final corner and started heading for the finish line, I could hear the crowd. Maybe I was envisioning that they were cheering just for me. *Whatever it takes!* I turned into some kind of cheetah at that moment, and suddenly, I found myself sprinting. Like 1 km to go, and I was on fire. Running like a pro. *What the?* Then I crossed that finish line and vomited into a garden.

I could barely walk for more than three days and felt so sick that I could hardly eat. Seriously, who really enjoys this stuff? But I was still better off than my friend, who lost almost all of her toenails running that bloody marathon!

And then… Besides being a marathoner (a one-hit wonder), I was aiming to be an elite cyclist (Yep, also a one-hit wonder). Well, actually, there were two rides, one per year. My team and I often did charity events together, such as 50 km walks and half marathons (the marathons we did in relay mode, so we only did 5 or 10 km each), and I wanted to do another charity event. I heard about the Ride to Conquer Cancer, a cycle of over 200 km through Sydney and finishing at Windsor. I had to get a bike and some of those shoes (cleats) and raise a few thousand dollars to enter.

The first year, I managed to fit in a couple of training rides. I think I got to about 20 km on one ride and 40 km on another. That was it. But I was quite fit at this time, and I knew I could manage the ride. It was extremely challenging, and certain sections were very hilly, but it was really enjoyable. I was so glad that I did it. That year, I rode in honour of a friend who was suffering from melanoma. The next year, sadly, after she had passed away, her 15-year-old daughter asked me whether she could do the ride with me that year for her mum. Being friends with my daughter, who is the same age, she decided she wanted to do it as well. It was a road ride, so I had to drag my poor gym buddy back in so she could help with the girls. At least her toenails had grown back by that stage.

We decided that we would register for the ride and set about fundraising. We raised over $10,000, which was an amazing achievement. Unfortunately for me, I had a reasonably serious back injury. I dealt with it for nine months, working the entire time. The L4/L5 discs were severely herniated, completely compressing my sciatic nerve to the extent that the pain was travelling right down to my foot. I had two rounds of Cortisone injections, which didn't work. My neurosurgeon told me that I had to have spinal surgery within the next week.

The bike ride was in five weeks' time. I told him that this wouldn't work, but he didn't give me a choice and advised that post-surgery, I couldn't do anything exercise-wise for six months. I had committed to this ride, and I had to do it for the girls and for the people who had donated to our cause. But I went in for the surgery, and after a few days in hospital (I had some complications and had to stay a little longer than planned), I went home to recuperate.

I was back at work within a week and lined up on the start line with the other three girls a few weeks later. *Was I a little stupid? Yes, I probably was. Did it hurt? Yep! Do I regret it? No.* I knew that the girls couldn't do it without me, and it would be too much for my friend to manage the two of them on some of the roads we had to ride on. I made it the whole way, obviously doing my best to switch off the pain and almost crawling to the toilet in the break when I could hardly walk.

To make matters worse, I fell off the bike twice during this ride. I guess that's what you get when you haven't ridden for a year or physically trained for nine months. The second fall was the funniest and so much more embarrassing. I was sitting at a set of traffic lights, and for some reason, my brain didn't compute that I needed to get my cleat out of the pedal, so as I stopped, I proceeded to go crashing to the ground. Of course, I was surrounded by cars. The drivers and my daughter thought it was pretty funny once they knew that I was okay. But we did it. I was so proud of the girls and Gabby doing that ride for her mum. What an achievement for a 15-year-old.

Sometimes, we have to work through physical and mental pain when achieving goals. The best thing you can do for yourself is to stop saying, "I wish I could," and start saying, "I will." Then, do something about it. Preparing for and achieving these goals alongside my business goals kept me motivated, healthy, and focused. Each time you face up to and conquer situations that flare your fears and self-doubt, it builds your confidence, inner strength, and resolve to face things head-on. The next time you find yourself saying or thinking, "I can't do that," ask yourself, *Why? Why can't I do it?* All you'll hear are excuses you've made up. Because you can do it. It may take time, training, or preparation, depending upon what you want to do, but everything is impossible until it's possible, right?!

It takes a lot of brainpower, focus of the mind, and intellect to run a business and manage a team. So, undertaking physical challenges gave me a release of all the pent-up negative and stress-induced energy and brought in fresh, invigorating energy. As far as I'm concerned, pushing myself is just part of being a high achiever. When you set a goal, you make it happen. Any way possible. As I said, extreme exercise is my antidepressant!

CHAPTER 10

Honouring a Precious Memory

Sometimes, no matter how much love you have to give, it's just not enough. Just to add to the craziness of my life, I took in a foster child. This is a very tragic story and not one that I am at liberty to share too much about. But I want to tell you about her because she was a beautiful girl who unfortunately suffered too much in her lifetime.

She came to me when she was 13 years old. After ending up in Kiama, she became friends with my youngest daughter as she went to school and played soccer with her. Unfortunately, the lady she was living with at the time was unable to look after her and the other foster kids she already had.

We gave her everything and treated her like she was one of our daughters. She had her own room, I bought her clothes, we took her on holidays, she snowboarded for the first time, and we gave her as much love as possible. But over time, she just couldn't adjust or conform to a life with rules and normalcy. She went through stages of substance abuse, sneaking out at night, hanging around with a pretty bad crowd, and getting into fights at school. She was also committing self-harm (Sound familiar? Probably why I spent so much time trying, with everything I had, to help her). She ran away numerous times when things didn't go her way. Or when she wanted to go to a party, and we said no based upon past experiences of letting her do that. The police usually brought her back days later.

When things were good, they were very good with her, and I honestly thought that she may have been able to break through her past trauma and realise there was a much better life for her. She just needed to want it and be prepared to fight for it. But sadly, she lost her way again, and this time, when she ran away, she didn't come back. She had been with us for a little over a year. The things that these poor kids go through are more than any child should have to endure. I was desperate to help her understand that this was her opportunity for an amazing life.

Tragically, she passed away earlier this year. She had just turned 23 years old. It broke our hearts when we heard the news. I truly hope that she has found some peace now.

Fly high with all my angels, beautiful girl.

CHAPTER 11

The Art of Letting Go

After my mum passed, I felt quite lost and disjointed with everything I was doing. Not long after, my second husband and I separated after going on a family trip to Europe. Sometimes, blended families are difficult, and fly-in, fly-out relationships are very hard. Combining all of this with all that was and had happened in my life during this time, I was just completely empty.

I honestly felt like I had nothing left to give, emotionally, physically, or mentally. Which is not fair to anyone. My husband did his best to support me, but I was feeling like I couldn't breathe, and I just needed to break free from everything and everyone to try to find a way to put myself back together.

My girls were getting older and becoming a lot more independent. The business was in a really good place, and I had definitely nailed it with the dream team by then. But with the emotion of going through a second divorce as well as the grieving process all over again, it all just got too much for me.

I had reached most of my goals. I had multiple offices and an amazing team. I'd won leadership and business awards. I had reached the number one agent in the area (Source: Rate My Agent). I had succeeded and proved to myself that I could be a successful business owner. I had fulfilled my promise to myself and my daughters to never give up. It was time to try something new.

So, one day, I sat down with my entire team and discussed my thoughts about selling the business. They were incredible, 100 percent supportive of my decision, and promised to do everything they could to help with the process and ensure it went smoothly. We all cried together and promised to remain good friends, which we have to this day. This in itself made me so happy.

In business, there are often hard decisions to make, but I can honestly say this one was probably the hardest. Once I had their support and was totally transparent about my intentions, I spoke to my franchise group and did the same thing. Needless to say, they were also very supportive. They knew about most of my challenges during those years and gave me nothing but support throughout.

I tried very hard to sell within the franchise group, but that wasn't to be, so I sold to another group of amazing people who had an agency already in the area and wanted to expand. I sold the Berry office to my licensee in charge prior to the Kiama office sale. The purchasers of my Kiama business decided to keep everybody on, which sealed my decision to sell to them. This time, the sale went through as smoothly as I could have hoped for.

My exceptional property manager also took the time to personally contact and send the necessary paperwork to every landlord. We managed to get every management transferred over to the new company; the only three that we lost were due to the properties being sold or the owner moving into the property. I am super proud of how everything went this time around.

I guess you have to do it the hard way before learning the right way sometimes. Those learnings from my first business sale came in very handy. What is it that they say about the hardest learnings, often being the most powerful ones? *Phew.* I could finally let out the breath that I'd been holding all the way through this process. Hooray!

I wanted to do something special to reward my team for their support, love, and loyalty during this entire period. So, I took them all on an all-expense paid three-day cruise. We had the absolute time of our lives; it was such a perfect way to reward them and spend some fun time together before everything transferred over to the new owners. Appreciation, gratitude, love, and respect. I was so thankful and blessed to have been able to celebrate the sale with them.

CHAPTER 12

Uncharted Territory

Being a real estate agent and business owner in a small town has its perks, but it also has a lot of challenges. I was feeling completely suffocated after I sold the business. I just think it was hard being in a small town where everyone knows you and your business. I needed space to breathe. I needed anonymity. So, my solution at the time was to pretty much walk out of one life and into the next. Whether I was escaping from the world, searching for a fresh start, running away from pain and loss, or looking for answers to soothe my somewhat battered little soul, I don't really know. In all honesty, it was probably all of the above.

I loved being part of a community; the support that l received from most people there was wonderful. I will be forever grateful. But it was time for a change, and with my girls living their own lives, I knew I had to take a chance and go forth to see what lay ahead for me—just another leap of faith into the complete unknown.

Although moving away from my family and friends to an area where I only had one friend was incredibly hard—especially being an introvert—it was also quite scary. I bought a little apartment on the beach in the Northern Beaches of Sydney and spent the next two years basically doing road trips and lying on the beach. I renovated my apartment and took as much time as I needed just to get myself back into a space where I wasn't focused on other people's happiness and wasn't taking responsibility for anyone else but myself. The problem was that I found it extremely difficult to adjust to that. It seems I had spent my whole life being that distracted, busy, outer-world-focused person and not having to live within myself, my thoughts, my feelings, and my emotions.

How do I deal with this loneliness and my own company?

Don't get me wrong, though. I loved the freedom and the lack of responsibility and I loved having no agenda. I even loved being by myself— for a while.

But then something shifted, and suddenly, I felt like a fish out of water. Maybe it was because now I could totally let go, to release and express all the emotions I had been bottling up all those years. Maybe it was because I didn't know who I was without being someone everyone relied upon. Maybe it was pent-up guilt, regret, frustration, and anger about things that I had just accepted and hadn't spoken my truth about. Maybe I was just incredibly lonely after spending my life surrounded by people and missing my family. Whatever was going on inside resulted in me feeling totally lost. *Where did I fit into the world now? Who even was I? What was my life purpose now?*

In retrospect, I pretty much did the same thing I did as a teenager. I ran away. I isolated myself. I kept everything inside. I didn't ask for help. Instead, I just spent a lot of time crying.

But I truly believe that was exactly what I needed to do to release everything that had built up inside. I think I needed to remove myself from everything that was familiar to enable me to do that. I had to forgive myself for all the things that didn't go my way and appreciate myself for everything that did. I needed to let go of everything in my past that was stopping me from moving forward. I had to go deep within and heal from the inside out in a way that exposed all that I had covered up. Basically, I laid it all out, bare and naked as the day I was born. That was hard, and it left me feeling quite raw. But it was also the only way to process and let go of everything.

Sometimes, you need distance to see things more clearly. Because eventually, being in Sydney on my own had become a very empowering and confidence-building experience for me. Although I've always had strength and been very independent, I found an alternative inner strength and independence that I didn't know I had, one that allowed me to put myself first sometimes.

I fell into a new rhythm of being and started to look toward my next venture into business and self-development. But as always seems to happen, just as I was feeling like I had the world at my feet again and the sun was shining brightly on my life, there was one more wave. *Seriously?! How much drama can one attract in a lifetime?*

Being single was a choice that I had made because I needed time on my own before I could give time to somebody else. I was also very conscious of the hurt on both sides when relationships don't work out, and I wasn't really sure that I wanted to go through that again. But after many years of purposely staying single, eventually, loneliness started to sink in, and I decided to dip my toe in the water and see whether I was ready to be in a relationship again.

This little story is one that I have been tossing up whether or not I'm ready to share. I'm currently doing final edits and still having doubts about it being in here. But obviously, if you're reading it, I have put my big girl panties on and found the courage to leave it in.

It is something that I never thought would happen to me, and I guess it has definitely given me an understanding of how women can so easily end up in a situation like this.

I have never been one for online dating, but it seems to be the way everybody meets these days, so I decided that I should give it a go. I met somebody who lived very close by. We met up initially for a coffee and then had a few dates. They were good dates, too; we had a lot in common and fun whenever we caught up.

The fifth time we met, we went out with a friend. We were having an awesome night, but there was definitely too much alcohol and not enough food. Toward the end of the evening, we all got separated somehow. I found my friend, who was playing snooker with some people and wanted to stay, so I left to go and meet up with my date, who was waiting for me at another pub nearby. Because I had been drinking, I couldn't get in, so I tried to call him, but he didn't answer. I left a text message saying I would get an Uber home. He called back and was very angry and aggressive on the phone. He wasn't happy that I couldn't get into the bar.

I called an Uber and was waiting for it down near the beach, quite unsure about what was happening with him and why he had become so upset. Before it arrived, he called again and asked where I was, saying he was near the beach looking for me. I assumed that he had calmed down by then, so I walked over to where he said he was. But rather than having calmed down, he was even more aggravated. He grabbed hold of my arm and dug his fingers in so tightly that I had deep purple bruising covering the entire top part of my arm for weeks afterward. He was also yelling right into my face. I told him to let go and said that he was hurting me, but it wasn't until some people started walking over that he let me go. He started to calm down, which I thought was good as, unfortunately, my car and apartment keys were at his place. I had driven over there so we could get the Uber together.

I planned to go back there to get my apartment keys, get an Uber home, and pick up my car the next day. He followed me into the Uber when it arrived and seemed to be a lot more friendly. When we got back to his place, he couldn't find the house key that he had put in a pot plant next to the door. He was getting very agitated again, so I suggested that I have a look, as I had seen him put it there when we left. As I bent down to search for it, he suddenly grabbed me by the hair on the back of my head, pulled me backward towards him, and sputtered something into my face before he forcibly threw me face-first to the ground. He held me down as he was yelling at me, pushing my face into the grass. My instinct was to just freeze and not say a word, just to lay there as still as possible. Eventually, he let go of me, and the minute he did, I got up, and I ran. I didn't know the area well, but all I knew was that I had to get away, so I just kept running. I could hear him chasing me as he called out my name, so I hid in a laneway and got online to Uber.

It was around 2 o'clock in the morning, and I had no idea where I was. Luckily, I was able to use the map to pinpoint my location, and they turned up quite quickly. I had chunks of hair coming out where he had pulled it so hard, and I had a really sore neck for weeks afterward. I feel like the force with which he threw me to the ground gave me whiplash. You would think that being in that situation, you would want to run and tell everybody and get help. But I was numb. I just couldn't even verbalise it. I am a grown woman, I'm smart, I've travelled and lived alone, and I've been through a lot of hard things in my life. But nothing prepared me for this.

Dating is hard, especially for an older person who is searching for something deeper than just a fling. *But wowsers!! I didn't think it would be this hard!* I was starting to think that the universe really DID have it in for me! It was like two steps forward and five steps back. *Sheesh! How much can a girl take?!* But again, somehow, I picked myself up and dusted myself off, albeit over time. I can't say that I am completely back in the dating game, but I am building confidence and slowly beginning to trust again.

Let's hope that's the end of the traumatic experiences for me! Anyway, onward and upward was my only focus from that point on. I think that I was so used to crashing through these waves by then that I had a little more resilience and a lot more confidence in knowing that I could move past it eventually.

CHAPTER 13

A Wider Perspective

Back to business.

It's a much safer topic!

It was time for me to plan out my future and get started on the things that I had been passionate about for a long time. Even though the bloody 'Rona turned up around this same time, that wasn't going to stop me.

I had always loved mentoring, so I decided to set up a coaching business, which had been my ultimate mission since I left Kiama. I truly love giving back and helping people to achieve their goals, push through challenges, and give them the courage to go after whatever they want. I believe I have so much to give in this space and many experiences to share. I have found purpose in helping others through my work, and this newfound sense of meaning brings immense fulfilment—especially in helping women who want to build a future for themselves and their families.

The life lessons that I've embraced completely have strengthened my philosophy that failure is essential to the journey. If you haven't failed at something, you aren't trying hard enough. Failure was not an end, but a bridge to future success for me. The adversity I faced the first time in business made me work harder, smarter, and more confidently, knowing what to avoid and what to change. It gave me the ability to leverage every aspect of my first business to build a bulletproof foundation for the next.

I am sharing my experiences to help people shift from "I can't" to "I can!" through the creation of a resilient mindset for success. Because belief in yourself is crucial to your business journey, but it's something many people struggle with. Self-doubt is one of the biggest obstacles, and the ability to overcome it is one of those challenges that has held many back from achieving the goals and aspirations they have always dreamed about. But it is something that you can overcome with the right knowledge and support.

And once you do that, you'll know what it feels like to fly.

Although I had belief and confidence in operating and growing a business, I understood and accepted that I wasn't invincible. I needed to learn the significance of self-compassion, self-acceptance, and self-love in tough times rather than self-blame, self-sacrifice, and self-sabotage. The eventual realisation that it is okay to ask for help is one of my main motivations for speaking out and providing a solution for others who need some support and encouragement to be the best version of themselves that they can be.

This is now my fifth business, four of which have been start-ups. I've found that throughout the process of growth, the biggest challenge for most business owners (including myself) and people in sales or target-based roles is accountability. Strength lies not in isolation but in collaboration. It's hard being at the top or operating as a sole trader; you often feel alone and unable to find the right people to draw from. Staying motivated, on track, and focused on goals and objectives is something we need to work on regularly, as it's not a natural state of being for most. It's easy to fall into a pattern of second-guessing yourself and getting a little lost in the process.

We all need someone with an impartial viewpoint to run scenarios by, seek advice, talk through challenges, and who can keep us accountable for our ultimate desired outcomes—someone to help us stay the course and motivate us to take action as they stand by us. That's what I am now, your plus one in business.

Many start a business without necessarily having much experience in leadership and management or the knowledge to plan and map out their first two years in business. They don't understand how the required initial capital outlay is calculated, the monitoring of overheads, cash flow forecasting, or the implementation of recruitment planning, growth strategies, and how to build the framework of an integrated and sustainable culture with unparalleled customer experience.

Knowing how much the business leadership and management course helped me prior to setting up the second business, I have developed an online or face-to-face module-based start-up platform with an editable workbook that enables new business owners to learn, plan, build, and write their own successful business model and action plan. My Business Launch Pad provides an innovative solution to successfully starting a business.

I've also developed a performance and accountability app to help salespeople, property managers, business development managers, and principals record and keep track of their statistics and KPIs on a daily basis. With RePerform, you simply add in your annual targets, which will be automatically broken down into monthly goals and measurable KPIs to keep you on track. It only takes 5 to 15 minutes a day to complete your daily activity log. Business owners will be able to monitor individual and overall team performance, and it will highlight areas that your team may need additional support and training.

RePerform is due to be launched by the end of October 2023. You'll find it on the App Store or through my website, marniebeauchamp.com.

I am fortunate to work with many different types of sales and customer service-focused businesses, as well as real estate agencies.

If I can help you in any way, please simply reach out to me.

FINAL CHAPTER

Full Circle

As I write the final chapter of this book, I am enjoying a solo road trip through the beautiful Tasmanian wilderness. I'm sitting in front of a fire with a glass of red wine and admiring the stunning views out over Cradle Mountain. I am happy and grateful for my life's journey so far. I've survived some hardships and enjoyed many more incredible moments.

In the early days, when I lost everything, it was hard not to let self-doubt creep in. But the difference was I didn't allow it to stop me. I like to think of my life as a tapestry woven with threads of success and failure, joy and sorrow, resilience and vulnerability. I now see that setbacks are not synonymous with failure but rather opportunities for growth. They encouraged me to rise each time I fell and showed me the power of resilience. I learned an amazing amount from every single stage of my life, and although there have been things that I totally wish I could go back and do differently, every piece has played a part in shaping who and what I am today.

My daughters were my source of inspiration, and I wanted to show them the importance of pursuing their passions, even in the face of adversity. I've found solace and wisdom in the process of learning about myself. I still have a long way to go to find that eternal inner peace and unconditional self-love, but I'm so much more aware of what is happening inside me.

I take every opportunity to partake in new experiences and confront my fears. I'm living my life without regret, and I'm finally reflecting on what I have achieved.

I am once again living close to my family and my friends. Turns out that leaving was an essential part of my journey but not the final destination.

I purchased my 14th property this year, and although I've lost many through divorce and the court case, I still think that's a pretty good achievement—but I'm not done yet.

I've travelled the world, but I'm not finished with that yet, either.

I believe I've been successful in business, but the best is yet to come.

I have an amazing and supportive family and the best besties ever. My two beautiful daughters are my heart and my soul. I'm thankful they're healthy and happy and so loved. They deserve that and more. And I have the most wonderful, adorable, gorgeous little grandson! I am so in love with this little boy. *Yes, I'm a proud Ma.*

My current journey is one of giving, and I am committed to helping others achieve their dreams. I'm excited about the future in a way that I haven't been before. I find my strength in everyday life through gratitude and spending time in balance with my family, friends, and my clients.

When there is pressure, I tend to go back to these questions. *When is enough? What is enough?* Knowing that right now, what I have is enough and is all I need to bring me back to the present. It grounds me.

I appreciate everything I have and, more importantly, who I have in my life, which is truly all I have ever wanted or needed. My heart is full of love and accomplishment.

One more thing, in relation to genetics and driving: If you were paying attention in the first chapter, you'll recall my mention of this. We have a hereditary genetic eye disorder called Macular Dystrophy on my mum's side of the family.

My nan had it, my mum had it, my uncle had it, one of my brothers has it, and I have it. There is no cure, resulting in both my mum, my nan, and my uncle being declared legally blind. You don't go completely blind—but you can no longer read, determine distances, recognise faces, or drive, amongst other things—so I guess you're mostly blind. This condition has some weird aspects, so it's very hard to explain how it works, but as a base-level explanation, my direct vision disappears—I have to look next to something to be able to see it. For example, if I were to look straight at a black spot on a white wall, I wouldn't be able to see the black spot. Until I looked away. I rarely speak about it. I don't think about it. I don't accept it. But it's there, and it's getting worse. My mum had to give up her driver's licence at the age I am now. As did my uncle. But I refuse to give in.

Besides business and family, my passions are driving, travelling, and reading. So, I'm cramming in as much as I can while I still can. Maybe this book is also a big "F you" to that gene trying to take books away from me.

I'm doing a lot of healing meditation, fasting, and researching ways that I can overcome this naturally. There are many foods and natural, pure supplements that can boost our immune system and help our bodies' ability to repair and regenerate broken and damaged cells. Our bodies heal our wounds, so why can't mine fix this? I have to believe that it can.

Wish me luck!

To everyone reading my story, I hope you find solace in knowing that life is a journey that is rarely a smooth, linear path. Don't be afraid to dream big and reach for the stars, even if it means taking risks.

Our journeys, though unique, are forever intertwined by the shared experiences of life and business.

Surround yourself with those who lift you up, support you, and believe in your dreams. And above all, believe in yourself—believe that you have the power to rebuild or create anew, no matter how many times those waves knock you down.

THANK YOU FOR READING MY BOOK!

CLAIM YOUR FREE WELCOME CALL

Click the Link:

I appreciate your interest in my book, and value your feedback as it helps me improve future versions. I would appreciate it if you could leave your invaluable review on Amazon.com with your feedback. Thank you!

Made in the USA
Columbia, SC
28 October 2023

3fd21cd8-a6d5-4968-97f6-4be2dfb14fe8R01